SCARY BITCHES

AN ANTHOLOGY OF THE SCARIEST WOMEN YOU WILL EVER MEET

WILLIAM WEBB

Absolute Crime Press
ANAHEIM, CALIFORNIA

Contents

ABOUT ABSOLUTE CRIME

Absolute Crime publishes only the best true crime literature. Our focus is on the crimes that you've probably never heard of, but you are fascinated to read more about. With each engaging and gripping story, we try to let readers relive moments in history that some people have tried to forget.

Remember, our books are not meant for the faint at heart. We don't hold back--if a crime is bloody, we let the words splatter across the page so you can experience the crime in the most horrifying way!

If you enjoy this book, please visit our homepage to see other books we offer; if you have any feedback, we'd love to hear from you!

Dear reader, your heart may not be able to handle the shocking true facts presented in this humble volume. You have been warned.

INTRODUCTION

With all of the attention placed on murderers of the male persuasion, you may be under the mistaken impression that the fairer sex has little if any blood on their hands.

Sure, women have killed people over the years, but aside from a poisoning here and there, they couldn't have been that bad, right?

Wrong.

True, there have been fewer female serial killers than men (that we know of), but as this book shows the women who have taken part in this sickening pastime were every bit as twisted, cruel, and terrifying as their overhyped male counterparts.

From bathing in blood to baby-killing, the fifteen women profiled in this book have stories shocking enough to make even the toughest, creatine-guzzling he man faint.

ELIZABETH BATHORY: THE COUNTESS OF BLOOD

Countess Elizabeth Bathory de Ecsed was history's first celebrity serial killer and possibly the most famous serial killer of all time. Her story has inspired dozens of novels, movies, metal songs, video games, trading cards, comic books, and at least two operas.

Her biggest claim to fame is inspiring the story of Dracula and much of the modern vampire mythology. Novelist Bram Stoker supposedly used her story as the basis for his novel Dracula. More recently, numerous movies and television shows have linked her to Dracula himself, even alleging that Bathory was Dracula's wife. That, like much of the mythology that's grown up around her, is false:

Dracula died at least two centuries before she was born.

Even when shorn of the vampire mythology, Countess Bathory's story is still bizarre and entertaining enough to be a novel. When you read her life's tale, it's easy to see why people associate Countess Bathory with vampires. Even if she wasn't a legendary bloodsucker, she certainly behaved like one.

A Privileged Childhood

Elizabeth Bathory (Erzsebeth Bathory in her native Hungarian) really was a countess. Her family was also very important; one of her cousins, Stefan Bathory, was King of Poland and fittingly Duke of Transylvania (Dracula's homeland). Elizabeth was born in Nyibator, Hungary around 1561 and grew up in Ecsed Castle in Transylvania.

Countess Bathory was a wild young woman who may have suffered from mental illness. She apparently had a terrible temper and displayed incredible aggression. When she was 14, Elizabeth reportedly scandalized her family by getting pregnant by a peasant. When she was 15, Elizabeth got her title by marrying Count Ferencz Nadasy, a famous soldier who spent most of his time fighting the Turks.

As a girl, Elizabeth was linked to witchcraft; her aunt was reputed to be a witch and her uncle an alchemist and a devil worshipper. One of her nurses was later arrested for witchcraft and accused of sacrificing children in black magic.

The Crimes that Created a Legend

Countess Bathory was an important woman whose husband commanded the Army that defended Hungary from the far more powerful Turks. She had control of the Castle of Csjete, a castle on the main invasion route between the Ottoman Empire and Vienna, the capitol of the Austrian Empire.

Bathory was obsessed with beauty and her appearance. She spent hours admiring herself in mirrors and changed her clothing several times a day in an age when most people only owned one set of clothes.

It was this obsession with beauty that led to her crimes and reputation as the Blood Countess. She started luring peasant girls to her castle with promises of work as maids, then killed them, and according to legend, bathed in their blood. The idea was to keep Countess Bathory's skin looking young, but she may have been sacrificing them to the devil or a deity called Isten.

Later on, Countess Bathory, who could reportedly read and write four languages, established a finishing school for the daughters of the local gentry. Instead of teaching the girls manners, she murdered them as well. Later accounts indicated that she or her henchmen tortured and sexually abused the girls before killing them.

The abuse the girls were subjected to was particularly horrific. The victims were locked in a cellar and beaten until their bodies swelled up. The Countess often participated in the brutality herself and often had to change her clothes because she got blood on them. Some stories indicate that Countess Bathory's husband, Count Nadasy, also participated in the killing and torture when he wasn't at war.

The number of young women murdered by the Blood Countess is unknown, but some historians speculate the body count could reach as high as 650. If that is true, it would make her the greatest serial killer in history. She not only conducted killings at Csjeste, but also at her other estates in Hungary and even in Vienna.

Part of the reason Bathory was able to butcher so many victims was that she had lots of help. In addition to her husband, most of the servants at her castle apparently participated in the mayhem.

Countess Bathory's killing spree apparently went on unchecked from 1585-1610, a period of 25 years. The slaughter continued that long because she was a powerful and politically connected noblewoman. It finally took the intervention of the King of Austria to bring it to an end.

Trial and Sentence

By 1610, Countess Bathary's crimes had grown so blatant that King Mathias II of Austria (who was also King of Hungary) was forced to act. Mathias ordered Gyorgy Thurzo, the Palatine (or governor of Hungary), to investigate allegations that a Lutheran minister was making against the Countess. Thurzo moved slowly because of her family's wealth and power.

Interestingly enough, the government was afraid to execute Bathary because King Mathias had borrowed large amounts of money from her. The King would have had to pay this debt if the Countess had been executed, so he took other actions. Elizabeth was arrested and imprisoned for life and never placed on trial because a trial would have embarrassed the nobility. Four of Bathary's servants were tried, and three of them were burned at the stake as witches.

Elizabeth Bathory was placed under house arrest and locked up alone in the tower of her castle for four years. She was found dead on Aug. 21, 1614. Countess Bathory's reputation was already so bad that the local villagers refused to have her body buried there. Instead, her body is in her family crypt in her hometown of Ecsed.

She Lives on in Fiction

Countess Elizabeth Bathory died nearly 500 years ago, but she lives on in fiction and popular culture. Fictional versions of the Countess have battled such popular superheroes as Hellboy, Batman, and even Buffy the Vampire Slayer. In the real world, she has inspired a Swedish metal band called Bathory, Japanese Manga comics, and hundreds of metal songs. Even though she was not a vampire, the Blood Countess seems to be immortal.

AMELIA DYER: BABY FARM MURDERER IN VICTORIA'S ENGLAND

Victorian England wasn't a very friendly place for women who were poor, unmarried, and pregnant. It was even worse for the children of such women, particularly if they ran into a monster named Amelia Dyer.

Dyer was a baby farmer, a criminal that claimed to adopt unwanted children for a fee, but murdered them instead. Desperate women would pay Dyer between £5 ($8.13) and £20 ($32.51) to get rid of the babies. The standard practice of baby farmers was to let the children die of neglect, then pocket the cash. Dyer found this too slow, so she simply started killing the children directly.

Childhood

Amelia Dyer grew up in a lower middle class family in Pyle Marsh, England, which is now part of Bristol. Her father was a master shoemaker, and unlike most women in Queen Victoria's England, Amelia did learn to read and write. Amelia's mother suffered from a mental illness caused by typhus as a girl.

After her father's death, Amelia left home, served an apprenticeship to a corset maker, and married a man named George Thomas. She later became a nurse, but didn't stay in the nursing profession long after realizing that she could make more money from baby farming.

Dyer apparently turned to crime because George Thomas had died and she needed to support her daughter, Ellen. She turned to baby farming around 1869 and murder shortly afterwards. Dyer continued with the horrific practice for nearly 30 years.

Murdering Babies for Profit

Amelia Dyer first found her victims through a midwife named Ellen Dane. Dane eventually fled to America to escape prosecution for involvement in Dyer's crimes. Once Dyer was out of the picture, Amelia turned to another method; she placed ads like this one in newspapers: "Married couple with no family would adopt healthy child, nice country home, Terms £10 ($16.25)."

Ten pounds was a lot of money for an average person in Victorian England. The mother would pay Dyer the money thinking she would arrange an adoption. Dyer took the cash, but quickly disposed of the baby. Once she got the babies, Dyer would strangle them and dump them into a river, usually the Thames.

The worst aspect of Dyer's crimes was that she was able to get away with them for over 25 years. To make matters worse, Dyer was actually arrested for killing babies on two separate occasions. In 1879, a doctor she had hired to write death certificates turned her in. She pretended to be insane and was sent to mental hospitals twice.

Once she was released, Dyer went right back to murdering babies again. After being released a second time in 1893, she began simply killing the babies and dumping the bodies. That saved her the expense of paying a doctor to write a death certificate and made her crimes more difficult to detect. To make sure nobody heard the baby, she would strangle infants by using tape. Amelia made extra money from her crimes by pawning the clothing the babies had worn.

Dyer usually disposed of the bodies by placing the babies in a carpet bag, weighing it down with bricks, and tossing it into the Thames. It was this practice that finally led police to her through detective work worthy of Sherlock Holmes.

Captured by 19th Century Science

The police became aware that something was wrong when a package containing the body of a baby girl named Helena Fry was found floating in the Thames. The package was examined by Detective Constable Anderson, who discovered a label with the address of a Mrs. Thomas on it. Mrs. Thomas was an alias that Dyer was using.

The police put Thomas's home under surveillance and set up a sting operation to nail Dyer. They had a young woman approach her and ask about getting rid of a child. The ploy worked, and constables were able to get enough evidence to search the Thomas home. The cops didn't find any dead babies, but they did find the murder weapon (edging tape), pawn tickets for children's clothing, and paperwork linking Dyer to the adoption racket.

The paperwork found at the house showed that as many as 20 children had been placed under the care of Mrs. Thomas. None of the children could be found, so Dyer and her son-in-law, Arthur Palmer, were arrested on April 4, 1896. The police then dragged the Thames and found six more dead babies. Each of the babies had been strangled with white tape.

Once again, Amelia Dyer tried to beat the rap with the insanity defense. This time it didn't work, and she was convicted of murder on May 22, 1896.

Less than a month later, on June 10, 1896, Amelia Dyer was hanged at Newgate Prison in London.

After her arrest, authorities found evidence that indicated Dyer may have killed many more children. The total number of victims is unknown, but some historians believe she may have strangled as many as 400 children. Amelia's daughter, Polly, and son–in-law, Arthur, were initially charged as accomplices. They were never tried because Dyer confessed to all the crimes.

Amelia Dyer and Jack the Ripper

There is a popular school of thought that has tried to link Amelia Dyer with Jack the Ripper, who murdered prostitutes in London. The theory is that Dyer killed the prostitutes through botched abortions. There is no evidence that Dyer was an abortionist; instead, she killed babies after their birth. Even though she probably wasn't Jack the Ripper, Amelia Dyer may have been one of the most evil women who ever lived. She killed defenseless children in order to get her hands on small sums of money.

KATHERINE KNIGHT: AUSTRALIA'S CANNIBAL BUTCHER

Many killers have a reputation as butchers, but Katherine Knight really was a butcher. She worked as one and later used her skills on her only known victim.

Even though she cannot be considered a serial killer (she had only one recorded victim), the psychotic biker chick Katherine Knight is one of the most memorable killers in Australian history. Her claim to fame was stabbing, skinning, and decapitating her boyfriend, then cooking and eating parts of his body. If that wasn't bad enough, there is evidence that she planned to serve her victim's flesh to his own children in a meal.

Childhood and Married Life

Katherine Mary Knight had a long history of violence that dated to her childhood when she was
sexually abused by family members. By the time
she was in high school in New South Wales, Katherine was known as a bully who terrorized younger
children. She also picked fights with a male class-
mate and a teacher.

By the time she was 16, Katherine had dropped
out of school and gotten her dream job cutting up
the organs of dead animals at the local slaughterhouse. She was so proud of the knives she used at
the job that she hung them over her bed. When
she was 19, Katherine married David Kellet and reportedly tried to strangle him on her wedding
night.

After David left, Katherine threw her two-month
baby onto the railroad tracks in the hope that a
train would run over the girl. She also went into
town and threatened several people with an axe. A
few days later, Katherine slashed a woman in the
face with a knife and kidnapped her. She then took
a little hostage and threatened him with a knife.

Despite this violence, Katherine was never
jailed, and instead, spent time in mental hospitals.
The authorities even let her keep custody of the
daughter she had tried to throw in front a train.
Her psychotic behavior continued, though; she cut
the throat of a two-month-old puppy in front of her

new boyfriend, David Saunders. She also hit Saunders in the face with an iron and stabbed him with scissors.

By 1989, Knight had three daughters and a house. She decorated the house with animal skins, skulls, traps, boots, leather jackets, machetes, pitchforks, and even rakes. She later become involved with another man named John Chillingworth and had a son with him.

Cannibalism Down Under

In 1995, while involved with Chillingworth, Knight had an affair with a miner named John Price. She eventually moved in with Price and two of his children. Price eventually became Knight's only known murder victim.

The two stayed together until 1998 when Price refused to marry Knight. This upset the woman who made a fake allegation that Price was stealing from his employer. Price got fired and threw her out. Incredibly, the two got back together a few months later.

This was a bad move, because in February 2000, Knight stabbed Price in the chest. Price finally wised up and got a restraining order against her. The move was too late because Knight was already planning to kill him.

That night, Katherine entered Price's house with a butcher knife and stabbed him 37 times. After stabbing Price, Katherine skinned him and hung the skin up in his living room. She used the skills she had learned at the slaughterhouse to cut up the body and cook parts of it with pumpkin, zucchini, cabbage, squash, potatoes, and gravy. To add insult to injury, Knight set plates on the dinner table in order to serve Price's body to his own children. Interestingly enough, Knight didn't finish the meal she had prepared; instead, she threw the dish out into the backyard after eating part of it.

Fortunately, the kids weren't home because they were staying over with a friend. After preparing the meal, Knight apparently tried to kill herself by taking an overdose of sleeping pills. She also left a suicide note that falsely accused Price of raping her daughter.

Investigation and Trial

The day after he took out the restraining order, Price didn't come in for work. His boss sent a coworker to Price's house to see what had happened. The co-worker and a neighbor noticed blood on Price's front door and called the police.

When constables arrived, they broke down the door and found Knight unconscious in the home. They also found Price's skinless and headless body and evidence of the meal that Knight had prepared.

Knight tried to plead guilty to manslaughter, but the court rejected her attempt. Instead, she was bound over for a trial that never occurred.

Katherine Knight pleaded guilty to murder the day before trial was scheduled to begin. When she was sentenced, Knight became hysterical when details of her crime were read in court.

Katherine Knight was the first woman sentenced to life imprisonment without parole in the history of Australia. She is currently locked up at the Silverwater Women's Correctional Centre in Sydney. Knight's fellow prisoners include another notorious Australian serial killer, Kathleen Megan Folbigg, who is serving a 25-year sentence for killing her four infant children.

BEVERLY ALLITT: "ANGEL OF DEATH" IN THE HOSPITAL WAR

The scariest female serial killer of all might be Beverly Gail Allitt, a nurse who instead of caring for sick children, murdered or try to murder them. It is easy to see why Allitt was given the title "Angel of Death" by the tabloids.

The most frightening thing about Beverly Allitt is where her crimes were carried out – in the children's ward of the Grantham and Kesteven Hospital in Lincolnshire, England where she worked. Also disturbing was the fact that she targeted some of the most defenseless victims possible, including a boy with cerebral palsy and a seven-week-old baby.

Odd Behavior Leads to Murder

Beverly Allitt's behavior was odd from the start. When she was a girl, she faked injuries to gain attention. She even wore fake bandages and casts in an attempt to appear injured. As a teenager, Allitt was a hypochondriac who abused Britain's National Health System. She faked sickness in order to spend time in hospitals.

Beverly eventually became an expert at fooling doctors into thinking she was sick when she was really healthy. She got so good at this that she was able to convince a surgeon to remove a perfectly healthy appendix from her body.

When she got older, Allitt decided to make the National Health Service her career and trained as a nurse. During her nursing training, Allitt may have smeared feces on nursing home walls; no explanation for that behavior has been made.

The Angel of Death Goes to Work

Even though she flunked her nursing examinations, Allitt was still able to get a job at the National Health Service as a State Enrolled Nurse. Her first assignment was to Children's Ward 4 at the Grantham and Kesteven Hospital in 1991. The murders began almost as soon as she set foot in the ward.

The cruelest of these deaths was the first, seven-week-old Liam Taylor, a baby who suffered from respiratory problems. Allitt volunteered to care for

Liam, but turned off monitors that would have alerted other nurses to a problem. As a result, Liam suffered brain damage so severe that his parents decided to remove him from life support and let him die.

Over the next 59 days, three more children died under suspicious circumstances in Ward Four, and at least nine others were attacked or injured. One of them, one–year-old Kayley Desmond, died in the same bed where Taylor had been attacked. Most of the children suffered from heart attacks while under Allitt's care.

It isn't known how Allitt killed all of her victims, but she administered overdoses of insulin to two of them and a drug called Lignocaine to another. These drugs apparently came from the hospital's own pharmacy. Air bubbles, which indicate that air was injected into veins in an attempt to cause a heart attack, were found in the blood of another.

What is known is that Allitt's body count would have been much higher if it hadn't been for the professionalism of her co-workers. They saved the lives of several children who were victims of Allit's accidents.

Two of Allitt's victims were two-month-old twins Becky and Katie Phillips. Allitt murdered Becky Phillips with an insulin overdose. When Becky died, Katie was admitted to Ward 4 where Allitt tried to kill her with overdoses of Lignocaine and insulin. Katie lived, but suffered permanent brain damage and paralysis. Incredibly, Katie's parents had asked

Allitt to be Katie's godmother because of the "care" she had given Becky.

Investigating the Angel of Death

The high number of deaths and heart attacks in Ward 4 alarmed hospital authorities who launched an investigation. Eventually, a hospital consultant, Dr. Nelson Porter, found a high level of Lignocaine, a heart medication that is not supposed to be given to children, in the body of Claire Peck, who had died while under Allitt's care.

Police began investigating after Peck's death and discovered that Allitt was the only nurse on duty when all the children had died or suffered attacks. Allitt had access to the drugs suspected of being the murder weapon.

Allitt was charged with murder, attempted murder, and bodily harm, and found guilty of all charges on May 28, 1993. She was given 13 life sentences because of the heinous nature of her crimes. The magistrate at the trial recommended that Allitt serve a minimum of 40 years in prison, one of the longest sentences ever suggested by a British trial judge.

Nobody has ever been able to explain why Allitt turned on the children under her care. One popular theory is that she suffers from Munchausen syndrome, a mental illness that causes mothers to harm their children. This theory has never been proven.

The Angel of Death Today

Beverly Allitt is currently serving her life sentence at Ramptom Secure Hospital, a mental facility in England. She will be eligible for parole in 2022 when she is 54 because of a 2007 court ruling. In the last 10 years, Allitt has been the subject of two dramatizations on British television, one of which was a BBC movie called the Angel of Death.

Ilse Koch:
TheBeastofBuchenwald

Of all the war criminals produced in Nazi Germany, Ilse Koch was among the most loathsome. Her story is also among the most bizarre of all the stories about the Nazis. Koch is known in history as the Beast of Buchenwald, the Bitch of Buchenwald, and the Red Queen of Buchenwald for her activities at the notorious Nazi concentration camp.

Koch was so evil that even the Nazis couldn't stomach her activities and eventually stripped her of her powers. She later attracted worldwide media attention when she became the only Nazi war criminal to tell the war crimes tribunal that she was pregnant.

Early Life

The early life of the Beast of Buchenwald remains something of a mystery. Like many Nazis, she came from a fairly normal German working class background and lived a bland life before the war. Some accounts indicate that she was actually a polite and happy child.

What is known is that Ilse attended an accountancy course and worked as a bookkeeper for several years. She apparently joined the Nazi Party in 1932, shortly before Adolph Hitler came to power. In 1936, she became a guard and secretary at the Sachsenhasuen concentration camp near Berlin. In the same year, she married the camp's commandant, Karl Otto Koch. A year later, Karl was named commandment at Buchenwald and Ilse went to work there.

War Crimes and the Holocaust

Ilse Koch served at Buchenwald from 1937-1943, and in 1941 she was named an Oberaufseherin (or chief overseer) in charge of the female guards at the camp. Her biggest accomplishment at the camp was building a sports arena by using money stolen from the inmates.

It was Ilse's other activities that gave her the reputation as a monster. She apparently rode around the camp and whipped prisoners for fun. She was apparently involved in other activities, such as the starvation of prisoners, torture, and inhumane medical experiments.

The most gruesome story about Ilse is that she would select prisoners with tattoos for execution. Once they were dead, the prisoners would be skinned and their skin made into lampshades and other items. Some stories claim that Ilse even had a handbag made from human skin.

It also seems that Koch and her husband were stealing from the Nazis, as well as the inmates in the camp. On Aug. 24, 1943, Koch was arrested by the SS and charged with embezzlement and private enrichment. She was also charged with having prisoners killed in order to cover up her crimes. Koch's husband, who had moved on to run the Majdanek extermination camp, was also arrested at the same time.

Strangely enough, Otto Koch was later imprisoned in Buchenwald and executed there by his fellow Nazis in 1945 as Allied troops were advancing on the camp. The charges against Ilse Koch were dropped, and she was apparently drummed out of the SS. The reason the SS let her go was a lack of evidence, which seems far-fetched because the Nazis didn't care about evidence.

Fun and Games at the War Crimes Trial

Even though she escaped "Nazi justice," Ilse Koch couldn't escape from the Allies. The U.S. Army arrested her in June 1945 and put her on trial for war crimes in 1947. The trial was held before a U.S. military court at another infamous Nazi concentration camp, Dachau.

During the trial, Koch stunned the military tribunal when she revealed that she was eight months pregnant. The father of her baby is unknown, but it is widely believed that he may have been a U.S. Army officer of Jewish descent. The pregnancy didn't impress the tribunal, which sentenced her to life imprisonment for "violation of the laws and customs of war."

U.S. Army General Lucius D. Clay, who was then serving as governor of the American Zone in Germany, reduced Koch's sentence to four years of imprisonment in 1948. Clay said he made the move because there was no evidence that the lampshades were actually made of human skin. He claimed the shades were made of goat skin and the human skin story was made up by a reporter.

Even though he gave her a reprieve, Clay called Ilse Koch a rather loathsome creature. He also said he got more abuse for commuting Koch's sentence than anything else he did in Germany.

The Fate of a War Criminal

Koch didn't get off so easy; one of the first things the newly organized West German government did was arrest her in 1949. In 1950, the German government held a second trial, in which several witnesses testified that Koch had been involved in the making of lampshades from human skin, although no physical evidence that such lampshades had ever existed was entered in the proceedings. The prosecution eventually dropped the charges related to the lampshades.

Koch was eventually convicted of incitement to murder, incitement to attempted murder, and incitement to the crime of committing serious bodily harm to German and Austrian citizens imprisoned at Buchenwald. She was sentenced to life imprisonment and committed suicide at the Aichach women's prison in the German state of Bavaria in 1967.

Ilse Koch had two sons, one of whom reportedly committed suicide because he couldn't live with the shame of his mother's actions. Her second son, who had been conceived at Dachau and born at Aichach, didn't learn his mother's identity until he was 19 years old.

The strangest thing about Ilse Koch is, despite her reputation, there is no evidence that she actually killed anybody, even though she was present at a concentration camp where tens of thousands were murdered. The courts only ruled that she ordered others to kill for her. Even the most famous story connected to her, the human skin lampshades, has never been proven.

Even though most of the stories about her might be legend, Ilse Koch's memory lives to this day. She has been the subject of songs, including one written by Woody Guthrie, and movies, including the B-movie Ilsa, She Wolf of the SS.

BELLE GUNNESS: HOG FARMER AND BLACK WIDOW

Few serial killers were as imaginative or successful in the disposal of their victims as Belle Gunness was. Gunness owned a hog farm near La Porte, Indiana and apparently fed many of her victims to the hogs.

Gunness was an equal opportunity killer whose victims included her husbands, her stepchildren, her boyfriends, and at least two of her own daughters. The most reprehensible thing was that she did it all for money. When her killing spree began, Gunness collected insurance on her victims. Later on, she murdered many men simply for their money and even to steal carriages and horses from them.

A Murderer from Norway

Belle Sorenson Gunness was born Brynhild Paulsdatter Storeeth in Selbu, Norway in 1859. Little is known about her childhood, except that she grew up on a small farm about 60 kilometers south of Trondheim in Central Norway.

Gunness may have started her killing spree in the old country. According to an unconfirmed story, she attended a dance while pregnant and got kicked in the chest by a rich man. The kick caused Belle to abort her baby, and that changed her personality. The man who kicked her died shortly awards of unknown causes, which may have been poison. Gunness then spent three years working as a servant to get enough money to immigrate to America where her slaughter began in earnest.

Belle Gets Started

Gunness settled in Chicago and married another Norwegian immigrant named Mads Ditlev Anton Sorenson. The couple opened a candy store, which conveniently burned down within a year and provided them a large insurance settlement.

Some rumors indicate that Belle had four children at this time, all of whom died in infancy. The infants may have been poisoned because Belle collected life insurance settlements on at least two of them. Mads Sorenson himself conveniently died on July 30, 1900, the day on which Belle could collect two insurance policies on him. The first doctor who examined the body blamed the death on strychnine poisoning.

Gunness used the money she received from her husband's life insurance to buy a farm near

LaPorte, Indiana. Shortly afterwards, she married Peter Gunness, whose infant daughter died within a week of the marriage. Gunness, who was also insured, died in a "tragic accident" just six months after the marriage. Gunness's stepdaughter, Jennie, later told schoolmates that her mother killed her papa with a meat cleaver. Jennie was one of several victims whose remains were later found in Belle's hog pen.

The property Belle inherited from Gunness included a hog farm. She operated the farm with help from a hired man named Ray Lamphere. Belle Gunness began putting ads in the matrimonial sections of a newspaper looking for a husband. She advertised for a man of means.

Several suitors answered Gunness's ads, but only one of them escaped alive. The others simply disappeared as soon as Gunness got her hands on their money. Gunness, who was a huge strong woman, apparently beat the men to death and buried their bodies in her hog pen.

Detection and Escape of a Monster

Belle Gunness's activities were eventually exposed by her lover and hired man, Ray Lamphere. Gunness apparently fired Lamphere; who had helped her dispose of the bodies, in February, 1908. Lamphere started making accusations against her and threatening to tell Asle Helgelien, the brother of one of Gunness's victims, what was going on.

Two months after Lamphere was fired, Gunness's house burned to the ground and four bodies were discovered in the ruins. None of the bodies could be identified, but one was a headless woman. Several people that had known Gunness examined the body and said it wasn't her. Part of the reason they thought the body didn't belong to Gunness was that the body was no more than 150 pounds, and Gunness weighed more than 200 pounds. Later examination by doctors verified this theory, and an autopsy determined that the woman had been poisoned with strychnine.

It is highly likely that Belle Gunness got away and covered her tracks by murdering somebody else and burning down her own home. The local coroner disagreed because teeth identified as Gunness's were found in the ruins of her home.

After the fire, Gunness's new hired hand, Joe Maxon, told the local sheriff that Gunness had him cover holes in the hog pen with dirt. The sheriff had a local miner dig up the hog pen and dozens of bodies were discovered. Most of the bodies were never identified, but Andrew Helgelien (Alse's brother) and Jennie Olson were found.

Ray Lamphere was arrested, tried, and sentenced to 20 years in prison for his part in the murders. Lamphere died of tuberculosis in the state prison a year later.

Did She Get Away With It?

Two years after the fire, a clergyman named E.A. Schell came forward and claimed that a dying Ray Lamphere had told him how Gunness had got away. Schell said Lamphere had lured a woman from Chicago to work as a housekeeper. Gunness then murdered the woman and cut off her head. Gunness then dressed the woman in her old clothes and put her false teeth next to the corpse to fool authorities before torching the house and escaping.

Nobody knows if Belle Gunness escaped or not. Numerous sightings of her were reported over the years. She was seen in Chicago, New York, San Francisco, and Los Angeles. The last reports of her came in 1931, when one rumor had her living in Mississippi and another that Esther Carson, a woman arrested for poisoning a man for money in Los Angeles, was Gunness. Esther Carson died before she could be identified or tried.

Belle Gunness was also one of the world's most versatile serial killers. Lamphere later said she used numerous methods of killing, including poisoning, stabbing, and beating men to death. She was able to get away with it because of her size; she was over six feet tall and weighed nearly 200 pounds. That makes her one of the world's biggest female serial killers.

AILEEN WUORNOS: SERIAL KILLER AND PROSTITUTE

Aileen Wuornos was a small-time prostitute who became a national sensation in the United States when it was revealed that she had murdered seven of her customers. Like many serial killers, Wuornos was a career predator who engaged in many different types of crime.

Wuornos was also a second-generation predator. She never met her father, Leo Pittman, because at the time of her birth, he was in prison for the rape and murder of a seven-year-old girl. Pittman, a convicted child molester who was suspected of being a schizophrenic, hanged himself in Michigan State Prison in 1969.

A Horrible Childhood

Aileen Wuornos' childhood was a living hell; her father was in prison and she was abandoned by her teenaged mother. Wuornos was eventually adopted by her grandfather, who sexually assaulted her and regularly beat her. Wuornos also reportedly engaged in sex with her brother.

It is also easy to see why Wuornos hated men so much; when she was 15, she was raped by a friend of her grandfather. Because there was no abortion in the 1960s in Michigan where Wuornos grew up, the girl was placed in a home for unwed mothers. The baby was eventually placed out for adoption.

Wuornos reportedly started prostituting herself at age 11. By the time she was 15, Wuornos' grandfather threw her out of the house. Wuornos started supporting herself as a prostitute and living in the woods. She eventually traveled around the country and started getting into trouble with the law.

Between 1974 and 1987, Wuornos was arrested for a wide variety of crimes, including armed robbery, drunk driving, assault and battery, passing bad checks, and car theft, mostly in Florida. Wuornos was already a hardened criminal by the time she met and fell in love with Tyria Moore, a Daytona Beach hotel maid.

Woman on a Murder Spree

Aileen Wuornos graduated from street criminal to serial killer after meeting and moving in with Moore. She started killing her customers (or johns) and stealing their money.

The first victim was Richard Mallory, an electronics store owner from Clearwater, Fla. Mallory was also a convicted rapist, and Wuornos claimed she shot him in self-defense. Wuornos pumped Mallory full of bullets and left him dead in his car.

Over the next year, the bodies of five other men were found dumped on Florida highways. Most of the men were naked, and most of their bodies were full of bullets. The victims had little common, although most of them were older men around the age Wuornos' grandfather had been when he reportedly raped her.

The victims included Dick Humphreys, a former state child abuse investigator who had also been a Major in the U.S. Air Force and a Police Chief, a part-time rodeo worker, a sausage salesman, and a construction worker. In addition to killing the men, Wuornos apparently stole their cars and drove around in them.

These are the known victims; since Wuornos preyed on traveling men, there might be other victims who were never detected. The body of one of her suspected victims, Peter Siems, has never been found.

Captured by a Fingerprint

Aileen Wuornos was exposed and captured by her own clumsiness and arrogance. She drove around in the cars she stole from the victims, and then abandoned the cars after a period of time. Police found her fingerprint on the door handle of one of the vehicles that belonged to Siems.

Ironically enough, Wuornos and Moore dumped that car after getting into an accident on July 4, 1980. Witnesses that saw the accident gave police descriptions of Moore and Wuornos. The police were able to identify Wuornos because of her extensive criminal record.

Wuornos was eventually picked up by police at a biker bar in Volusia County, Fla. on Jan. 9, 1991. She was booked on an outstanding warrant for other crimes. By that time, she and Moore had apparently broken up. Moore was arrested the next day in Scranton, Penn.

Moore was able to keep herself out of prison by agreeing to testify against Wuornos. In spite of the betrayal, Wuornos kept calling Moore and asking for help. When Moore refused to withdraw her testimony, Wuornos confessed to the murders and started claiming she had killed the men in self-defense.

The trial attracted a lot of attention because of Wuornos' defense. She was convicted of the murder of Richard Mallory on Jan. 27, 1992. When the self-defense strategy didn't work, Wuornos' attorneys introduced evidence that showed she had been diagnosed with borderline personality disorder and antisocial disorder. The idea was to protect Wuornos from the death penalty, but it didn't work; she was sentenced to death five times.

Execution and Immortality

The appeal of Wuornos' death sentence dragged on for 12 years. The Florida Supreme Court, the U.S. Supreme Court, and Florida Governor Jeb Bush (the brother and son of the two presidents) rejected her appeals. Wuornos' was executed by lethal injection on Oct. 9, 2002. She was only the second woman ever executed in Florida.

Public fascination with Wournos was driven by two documentaries made by U.S. filmmaker Nick Brookfield after her death, Alien Wuornos: The Selling of a Serial Killer and Aileen: Life and Death of a Serial Killer. These documentaries inspired the movie Monster, which earned Charlize Theron an Academy Award for playing Wuornos. Other media inspired by Wuornos includes a TV movie, an opera, a song by Jewel, and strangely enough, several poems.

Mary Ann Cotton: England's First Serial Killer

Mary Ann Cotton was Britain's first celebrity serial killer. She gained her celebrity status because she went on her killing spree at the right time, the early 1870s. It was an age when rising literacy and new printing technology created mass-circulation newspapers for the first time. The newspapers needed something to print and attract readers, and serial killers were sure to do just that.

Mary Ann Cotton is particularly reprehensible because she killed her own family, as well as strangers. Her victims included her husbands, her own mother, her stepchildren, her lover, and her own children. Her weapon of choice was a common one in her era, poison, usually arsenic.

Childhood and Early Life

Mary Ann was the daughter of a miner named Michael Robson. She was born in Sunderland, England and grew up in Devon. Her childhood was marred by the death of her father, who fell down a mine shaft. Mary Ann was something of a loner who didn't get along with either the children at school or her stepfather, George Scott.

Like many working class girls in Victorian England, Mary Ann worked as a servant and trained as a dressmaker after leaving home. When she was 20, Mary Ann married a laborer named William Mowbray and moved to Plymouth. They later moved to Northwest England, where life was tough; four of their five children died.

Poisoning for Fun and Profit

Mary Ann's career as a murderer probably began in 1865 when William died of an unknown stomach disorder. Whether William's death was natural or engineered by his wife is unknown. What is known is that Mary Ann collected a life insurance claim for £35 ($56.89). This doesn't sound like much to us, but in 1865, it would have taken several months for the average English laborer to earn that sum.

Mary Ann lost no time in finding another husband; she married an engineer named George Ward on Aug. 28, 1865. Ward died a little over a year later, and once again, Mary Ann collected life insurance money on a dead husband.

Now an experienced predator, Mary Ann had already picked out her next victim, James Robinson. She went to work as Robinson's housekeeper right after George Ward died. Shortly after Mary Ann went to work at the Robinson house, Robinson's baby died. It isn't known if the baby perished of natural causes, but with Mary Ann in the house, it is doubtful.

Mary Ann's next murder was the most loathsome of all; she apparently poisoned her own mother. Mary Ann's mother was ill and asked her daughter to come stay with her in the spring of 1867. Her mother started getting better, but began complaining of stomach pains and died nine days after Mary Ann came to stay. Stomach pains are a well-known symptom of arsenic poisoning.

A few weeks after Mary Ann's mother died, her daughter, Isabella, and two of Robinson's children developed similar symptoms and died. Despite the suspicious deaths, Robinson married Mary Ann, who gave birth to another child, Mary Isabella, a few months later. Mary Isabella soon died after developing a stomach ailment.

Robinson finally threw Mary Ann out when he discovered that she had been stealing from him.

He also learned that she had forced his children to pawn his possessions.

Mary Ann Robinson found herself homeless and on the street. Predictably, she found another man to prey on. She met a man named Frederick Cotton, who lived with his sister, Margaret. Cotton was a widower and Margaret cared for his children. Shortly after Mary Ann arrived, Margaret died from a stomach ailment.

In 1870, Mary Ann illegally married Frederick Cotton and gave birth to a son, Robert, shortly afterwards. By 1871, Frederick had died of gastric fever. His two sons, Robert and Frederick Jr., died the next year. Mary Ann Cotton had taken out life insurance policies on all three. A man named Joseph Nattrass, whom she was having an affair with, died shortly after. Nattrass had just rewritten his will in Mary Ann's favor.

Greed was her Downfall

Shortly after Nattrass's death, Mary Ann became acquainted with Thomas Riley, an assistant coroner (the official who investigated suspicious deaths). She asked Riley if he could put her surviving stepson, Charles Edward Cotton, in the workhouse (a forced labor camp for the poor). Mary Ann even told Riley that she hoped Charles Edward would soon die so she could collect his father's money.

Riley refused to go along with Mary Ann's vile plan and became suspicious. When Charles Edward died five days later, Rile went straight to the police and asked for an investigation. This tripped up Mary Ann because it meant no death certificate would be issued and she couldn't collect the insurance money.

The investigation was soon picked up by the newspapers. Reporters investigated and learned of Mary Ann's past, including the two dead previous husbands.

The media coverage prompted the authorities to test samples of medicine Mary Ann had given Charles. The samples tested positive for arsenic, and Mary Ann, who was pregnant with her 13th child, was arrested.

Hanging and Nursery Rhymes

Like a true psychopath, Mary Ann Cotton insisted that she was innocent and she was the victim of persecution. At her trial, her defense was that Charles Cotton had died from inhaling arsenic found in the wallpaper of her home. The jury didn't believe it and found Cotton guilty. After an attempt to get clemency, Mary Ann Cotton was hanged on March 24, 1873.

After her death, Mary Ann Cotton was immortalized by two nursery rhymes. Incredibly, the Victorians thought that serial killers were an appropriate subject for children's music. Most of the rhymes start with "Mary Ann Cotton, she's dead and forgotten."

GERTRUDE BANISZEWSKI: THE TORTURE MOTHER

Even though her name is in the ranks of female serial killers Gertrude Baniszweski only murdered one person. That murder was so horrific that it was called the single worst perpetuated crime against an individual in the history of the state of Indiana. That's saying a lot because Bell Gunness also called Indiana home.

The most disturbing thing about Gertrude Baniszewski was her ability to enlist others in her crime. She was able to talk her own children and many of her neighbors' children into helping her torture, mutilate and murder Sylvia Likens, a teen-aged girl she had taken in as a border.

Girl Next Door to a Monster

Gertrude Baniszewski was born Gertrue von Fossan in Indianapolis in 1929, the year of the stock market crash. Life was tough during the depression and it got tougher when 11 year old Gertrude watched her father die of a heart attack. After her father's death Gertrude frequently fought with her mother.

When she was sixteen Gertrude married John Baniszweski, an 18-year old policeman. She stayed with Baniszweski for ten years even though he frequently beat her up. Even though the marriage failed it produced four children. Gertrude then married a man named Edward Guthrie but the marriage only lasted four years. After Guthrie she remarried Banisweski and had two more kids by him.

After leaving Banisweski for a second time, Gertrude lived with a man named Dennis Lee Wright for a time. Wright was 23 and Gertrude was 37. Wright left town after Gertrude gave birth to his child. Gertrude stayed in the working class area of Indianapolis where she had grown up.

Torture and Mutilation as Family Fun

After Wright left, Gertrude took to calling herself Mrs. Wright to cover up the fact that her son was illegitimate. She was also broke and had seven children to support. Since neither of her husbands was very good about sending the child support check, "Gertrude Wright" looked for ways to support her family.

One of them was taking in two of the children of a man named Lester Likens. Likens needed somebody to care for his kids because he worked out of town in traveling carnivals. His wife was unavailable to care for the children because she was in jail. Gertrude offered to take Likens two daughters Sylvia and Jenny in for $20 a week.

The arrangement didn't work out because Likens didn't send the $20 as promised. Baniszweski became enraged and had the Likens' girls beaten for stealing candy. For unknown reasons Gertrude hated Sylvia and began targeting her for abuse. Gertrude made her children push Sylvia down the stairs and beat her.

If that wasn't bad enough she had neighborhood children and her children's classmates come in and beat Sylvia as well. Gertrude even forced Jenny Likens to hit her own sister. To make matters worse Baniszewski began accusing Sylvia of being a whore and calling her filthy.

When Sylvia became unconscious, Gertrude locked her in the basement. Sylvia was kept in the basement naked and Gertrude began starving her. Gertrude also tortured Sylvia by pouring scalding water on her. When Sylvia suffered burns Gertrude rubbed salt into the wounds. Gertrude and her twelve year old son John Jr. also made Sylvia eat her own feces.

The horror was made even worse by the fact that Sylvia's older sister and a social worker visited the home where Sylvia was being tortured. The older sister, Diana Likens came over because Sylvia's sister Jenny had contacted her. Diana contacted social services which sent a social worker to investigate.

Gertrude told the social worker that Sylvia had run away. She also frightened Jenny into lying to the social worker by saying she would join Sylvia in the basement if she revealed the horrors going on in the home. The social worker returned to her office and filed a report recommending that follow up visits be made to the Wright home.

The nightmare reached a crescendo on October 21, 1965, when Gertrude ordered her children John, Stephanie and Coy to bring Sylvia up from the basement. Sylvia was tied to a bed and unable to leave. The next morning Gertrude, angered that Sylvia, who couldn't leave the bed, had wet it, stuck a Coca-Cola bottle into her vagina.

She then tried to brand the words: "I'm a prostitute and proud of it" on Sylvia's chest with a hot sewing needle. When Gertrude couldn't finish the work she ordered a local boy named Roy Hobbs Jr. to do it.

Murder and Detection

The horrors continued for two more days. Gertrude first proposed having John and Jenny take

Sylvia to the dump and leave her to die in the garbage. Sylvia heard this and tried to escape. Instead she was caught and thrown in to the basement. On Oct. 24 Sylvia and a boy named Coy Hubbard viciously beat Sylvia with a broomstick and a paddle.

The death came on Oct. 26 after Gertrude had the child give a fully clothed Sylvia a bath. When they took her out of the tub she was dead. This finally prompted Stephanie to tell Hobbs to call the police. When officers arrived Gertrude tried to fool them with a fake letter claiming that Sylvia had run away.

Jenny Likens then told police she'd tell them everything if they got her out of there. The cops listened to her and arrested Gertrude, three of her children, Richard Hobbs, and Coy Hubbard for murder. Four other children were arrested for assault.

She Died a Free Woman

Incredibly, Gertrude Baniszewski died a free woman. She was found guilty of first degree murder and sentenced to life imprisonment in 1966. In 1971 the Indiana Supreme Court ruled that media coverage had prejudiced the jury so Gertrude needed a new trial. Gertrude was again sentenced to life imprisonment.

Strangely enough Gertrude Baniszewski became a model prisoner who earned the nickname "mom" from younger inmates. By 1985 she was up for parole and despite 40,000 petitions demanding she stay in prison, Gertrude Banisweski was paroled and allowed to move to Iowa. In Iowa, karma in the form of lung cancer gave Gertrude the punishment she deserved she died on June 16, 1990 at the age of 60.

Gertrude's daughter Paula was found guilty of second degree murder in the case. Paula was released from prison in 1972 and moved to Iowa. In October 2012 it was revealed that Paula Baniszewski, using the name Paula, was working with special needs students as a teacher's aide. When school officials learned of Paula's true identity they quickly fired her.

IRMA GRESE: THE BEAUTIFUL BEAST OF BERGEN BELSEN AND THE HYENA OF AUSCHWITZ

Irma Grese's career as a guard and warden at notorious Nazi concentration camps, including Auschwitz and Bergen Belsen, was short, but notorious. She worked at the facilities for less than two years, but her crimes were horrific enough to convince a British military tribunal to sentence her to death.

Among the duties Grese had at Auschwitz was selecting the women sent to their deaths in the gas chambers. At the height of her powers, Grese was in charge of 30,000 female prisoners. She used her power at the camps to make life in them even more hellish for prisoners in that horrific environment.

Background

Irma Grese was a failure in ordinary life. She did poorly in school and had few friends as a girl. Instead, she lived for the League of German Girls (the Hitler Youth's program for girls). Little is known of her background, except that she was born in Wrechen, Germany in 1923 and her mother committed suicide when she was 13. Her father, Alfred, was a worker in a dairy and a member of the local Nazi Party.

After dropping out of school at 14, Grese worked at menial jobs, including a nurse's assistant and a helper in a dairy. She eventually found her dream job in 1942 when she enlisted in the SS and began training as a concentration camp guard. She reported for duty in 1943 and started outdoing the male Nazis for cruelty and terror.

The War Crimes of Irma Grese

Irma Grese used all of the power given to her by the Nazis to make life hell for the mostly Jewish women under her "care." The testimony against her at the Belsen Trial conducted by the British Army reads like a list of all the horrors of the Holocaust.

Witnesses alleged that Grese went out of her way to torture and kill women on their way to the gas chamber. Perhaps her greatest cruelty was to starve and brutalize dogs and deliberately sic them on prisoners. Grese also regularly shot prisoners and beat some prisoners to death with a whip.

Grese acted like a character out of a B-movie at Auschwitz; she wore high boots and carried a whip and a pistol. Grese apparently wore stylish clothes and large amounts of perfume and went out of her way to look pretty as a means of taunting starving wretched female prisoners. One prisoner even alleged that Grese deliberately selected beautiful women and sent them to the gas chamber.

Escape, Capture and Execution

By January 1945, Irma Grese was serving as a senior supervisor at Auschwitz in charge of 30,000 prisoners. Yet her power was shortlived because the Russian Red Army soon overran Auschwitz. Grese fled first to the Ravensbruck Concentration Camp, then to the Bergen-Belsen Concentration Camp in Germany.

In His Majesty's Custody

On April 17, 1945, Grese and the other SS personnel at Bergen-Belsen surrendered to His Majesty's Army. The British held Grese until Sept. 17, 1945 when she and 45 other war criminals were put on trial before a court-martial. After a 53-day trial, Grese was found guilty of war crimes and sentenced to hang.

A reporter for the British newspaper The Daily Mail reported that Grese and another war criminal, Elizabeth Vonkerath, were laughing and singing Nazi songs the night before their execution. Grese, who was extremely vain, was apparently trying to improve her appearance by making hair ribbons from rags.

Grese was hanged at Hamelin Jail on Dec. 13, 1945 by Albert Pierrepoint, who was considered the most efficient executioner in British history. Pierrepoint reportedly hung more than 400 people in his career, half of whom were Nazi war criminals. Pierrepoint was so famous that his exploits were dramatized in a 2005 film called Pierrepoint: the Last Hangman. Pierrepoint also hanged one of Britain's most notorious serial killers, the "Acid Bath Murderer" John George Haigh.

Inspiring Hatred

Like many girls in the 1940s, Irma Grese apparently had ambitions of becoming a movie star after the war. She didn't achieve that ambition, but she inspired hatred in those that she met. British war hero Eric Brown called her "the worst human being that I have ever met."

Holocaust survivor Olga Lengyel was so horrified by Grese's activities that she focused a large portion of her memoirs on the monster. Lengyel, who had been at Auschwitz under Grese's supervision, recorded that Grese reportedly had an affair with another notorious Nazi, Josef Mengele, the sadistic doctor that performed cruel experiments on inmates at Auschwitz. Unlike Grese, Mengele fled Germany after the war and lived for decades in hiding in South America.

Lenygel believed that Grese, who was having affairs with several SS men, became pregnant at Auschwitz. Rather than let pregnancy interfere with her cruelty and sadism, Grese forced an inmate doctor to perform an abortion on her in the camp. The fate of the doctor isn't known, but it's likely that Grese sent him to the gas chamber or shot him to cover up the fact she had an illegal abortion.

Irma Grese hasn't achieved as much fame as another female Nazi, Ilse Koch, but she earned a number of fearsome nicknames. They included Nazi She-Devil, The Beast of Belsen, The Hyena of Auschwitz, and The Beautiful Beast. Her story helped inspire the B-movie Illsa, She Wolf of the SS and several comic book super villainesses.

KARLA HOMOLKA: CANADA'S KILLER BARBIE

Karla Homolka was not only a reprehensible killer, but the crimes she committed with her husband, Paul Bernardo, turned an entire nation upside down. The blonde-haired veterinary assistant who was called Barbie by the press looked like an innocent girl next door, yet she became a key player in the most notorious crime in Canadian history.

The most loathsome part of the story is that Homolka helped Bernardo rape and murder her own sister Tammy. Homolka not only acted as Bernardo's accomplice, but she stole drugs that enabled him to get away with the crime. Like many accomplices in serial killings, Homolka later turned on her partner-in-crime in exchange for a lighter sentence.

Girl Next Door to Serial Killer's Assistant

Before she became a serial killer, Karla Homolka was known as a bright, beautiful, intelligent, and popular girl in her hometown of St. Catharine's, Ontario. She was also known for her love of animals, which prompted her to start work at a veterinary clinic in high school.

Karla's turn to the dark side began when she met a 23-year-old petty criminal named Paul Bernardo at a restaurant near Toronto. Bernardo's hobbies included sadomasochism, which Karla willingly participated in. The two married soon after, even though Karla was just 17, under the legal age of consent in Ontario.

Bernardo was a sexual predator who dabbled in other crimes, such as selling untaxed cigarettes. Bernardo also sold Amway products and became notorious as the Scarborough Rapist, who committed dozens of vicious sexual assaults on women in Toronto's suburbs between 1987 and 1990. During the rapes, Bernardo often terrorized his victims with a knife.

From Serial Rape to Murder

Paul Bernardo decided to curtail his activities as the Scarborough Rapist after being questioned by police. He moved to St. Catherine's and spent most of his time with Karla's family. Paul told the Homolka family that he was working as an accountant when he was really supporting himself by smuggling cigarettes from the U.S. High tobacco taxes in Canada make cigarette smuggling a profitable activity in that country.

Karla's involvement in Paul's activities began on July 24, 1990 when she laced spaghetti sauce with valium and fed it to her sister Tammy. Tammy lost conscious, which enabled Paul to rape her. Paul was obsessed with Tammy because he thought she was a virgin. Karla watched the rape and helped cover it up. Forensic evidence indicates that Tammy's face may have been burned with chemicals during the assault.

Tammy eventually died of a valium dose right after the rape. Karla covered up the crime by vacuuming the house and washing the sheets before calling 911. Tammy was taken to the local hospital where she was pronounced dead. Incredibly, the local coroner ruled Tammy's death an accident. The crime was particularly vile because the two had murdered Tammy in the Homolka family home.

Partners in Crime

Bernardo's next victim was Leslie Mahffy, whom he kidnapped off the streets of Burlington, Ontario, on June 15, 1991. Bernardo brought the 14-year-old home and told Homolka that the two now had a playmate. Karla and Paul then videotaped each other torturing and sexually assaulting Mahaffy. The girl was tied up during the assault and the two played Bob Marley music during the torture. After they were done with Leslie, Karla fed her a lethal dose of the drug Halicon, which she had stolen from her workplace.

If that wasn't bad enough, the two left Mahaffy's body in their basement while they had Karla's parents over for dinner. After the dinner, the couple dismembered the body with a circular saw, encased it in cement, and tried to dump it in a nearby lake.

Karla was even more involved in the next murder; she and Bernardo drove around St. Catharine's on April 16, 1992, looking for victims. They spotted Kristen French outside of a local Catholic high school. Homolka went up to French with a map and pretended to ask for directions. Bernardo then sneaked up on her behind and used a knife to force into the car. Karla held her down while they drove home.

Once home, the two tortured and abused French for three days straight over the Easter weekend. After they were done with French, Homolka beat her with a rubber mallet. The girl was then strangled, after which Homolka cut her hair to keep police from identifying her. French's naked body was dumped in a ditch in Burlington.

Slow Moving Police and Suppression of Free Speech

Incredibly, police were well aware of Paul Bernardo and Karla Homolka before the killings began. Records indicate that detectives interviewed the two several times in connection with the Scarborough Rapist investigation. They even took a sample of Bernardo's DNA and questioned the two about Bernardo's stalking of women.

Cops only moved on Bernardo when his DNA was matched to the Scarborough Rapist. Police placed Bernardo under 24-hour surveillance and interviewed Homolka in early 1993. By then, the two had broken up because Paul had beaten Karla with a flashlight. Karla had even charged Paul with domestic violence.

Paul was finally arrested on Feb. 17, 1993, over two years after he had been first questioned. Police executed search warrants and found videotapes of the crimes.

A Miscarriage of Justice

Homolka next proved herself to be a complete psychopath by accepting a plea bargain and agreeing to testify against Bernardo. Homolka received a 12-year sentence because she pleaded guilty to manslaughter instead of murder.

What happened next raises questions about Canada's status as a free country. The prosecutor asked a judge to impose a publication ban. That effectively meant reporters couldn't report on the trial or the plea deal in Canada. Lawyers said the ban was sought to protect Bernardo's "right to a fair trial," but cynics said prosecutors were attempting to cover up their own questionable actions.

The ban failed because American media, protected by the First Amendment, reported on the trial. Details of the events circulated widely on the internet and in the American media. Interestingly enough, the ban stayed in effect as late as 2000 and prevented the airing of an episode of Law & Order in Canada.

Bernardo was convicted of first-degree murder and aggravated sexual assault and sentenced to life in prison on Sept. 1, 1995. During the trial, Bernardo maintained that Homolka committed the murders. He has since stated she killed the girls to eliminate witnesses.

Escape to the Caribbean

Karla Homolka was released from prison in 2005 and disappeared from public view. She is currently living on the Caribbean island of Guadeloupe under the name of Leanne Bordelais. Canadian journalist Paula Todd reported that Homolka is currently married to a man named Thierry Bourdelais and that she has three children.

Even though Karla may have gotten away with her crimes, she will probably never receive a pardon. In 2010, Canada's Public Safety Minister Vic Toews announced that his government would ask parliament for a law making it illegal for notorious offenders to get pardoned. Toews made the announcement after newspapers reported that

Homolka would be soon eligible to receive such a pardon.

ROSEMARY WEST: CROMWELL STREET MURDERER

Rosemary West is one of just two British women sentenced to life in prison in modern times. When you look at her crimes, it is easy to see why; she helped her husband murder her own daughter and bury her body in the garden.

The stepdaughter, Heather West, was only the latest of at least 11 young girls that Fred and Rosemary West murdered in a crime spree that lasted nearly 25 years. Fred and Rosemary West were hardly good neighbors; he was a lifelong sexual predator and she was a prostitute.

A Horrible Childhood

Rosemary West's childhood in England was a living hell. Her father, William Andrew Letts, was reportedly schizophrenic and her mother suffered from mental illness, including depression. William Letts also reportedly beat and sexually abused Rosemary.

When he wasn't abusing Rosemary Letts, he reportedly demanded absolute obedience from his kids. His punishments included pouring cold water over his children. The children weren't allowed to play or even talk with other kids.

Rosemary (or Rose) was not a very bright girl; she did badly in school. She also learned to survive by doing whatever her father told her. Later on, it was alleged that Rose was having an incestuous affair with her father.

Marriage to a Sexual Predator

When she was 16, Rosemary met Fred West, who was living at a local caravan park (trailer park). West was a longtime rapist and petty criminal who had already raped and murdered at least two women before hooking up with Rosemary. West, who was 12 years older than Rosemary, already had a daughter from a previous marriage at the time of their "wedding."

The life of the West family was certainly bizarre; press reports and books indicate that Rosemary supported the couple by working as a prostitute.

Her customers may have included her father, who may have also molested Rose's stepdaughter, Anne-Marie, at the same time. In 1973, the couple was arrested for kidnapping a woman named Caroline Roberts and sexually assaulting her. Incredibly, they were fined for something called indecent assault and released.

The Murders

Rosemary West joined Fred's murder spree shortly after their wedding. Rosemary's first victim was her husband's daughter, Charmaine West, who was buried at the family home. This was one murder for which Fred had a good alibi; he was serving a prison sentence for theft when Charmaine was killed in 1971.

When Fred got out of prison, he helped his wife kidnap, sexually assault, and murder up to 10 teenaged girls. After Fred and Rosemary were done with the girls, they were dismembered and buried in the couple's cellar. Forensic evidence indicates that the Wests cut the girls' fingers and toes off before burying them, possibly in an effort to hide the girls' identity.

The most disturbing feature of the crimes is that the Wests had young children living with them in the home during the murder spree. Rosemary was also reportedly pregnant with some of her children while the murders were going on. At the same time he was murdering teenaged girls, Fred was also molesting his own daughters.

In 1986, the Wests committed the most heinous crime of all. Their daughter Heather stood up to Fred by resisting his sexual advances. Worse, she told a friend about her parents' activities. Afraid that Heather might go to the police, Fred and Rosemary murdered Heather and buried her body in the garden. Their son Stephen was forced to help dig the grave.

Finally Detected after 20 years

The Wests' house of horrors at 25 Cromwell St. in Gloucester, England was finally detected in 1992 when West reportedly filmed himself raping another one of his daughters. The daughter told a friend who told her mother, and the mother went straight to the police.

Fred and Rosemary were arrested and charged with rape and child cruelty on Aug. 6, 1992. The Wests' children were finally removed from the "home" and placed in foster care. The rape charges were dropped, but the Wests were now on the police radar. It was at this time that Detective Constable Hazel Savage searched the house and started asking questions about Heather West's disappearance.

Savage was convinced something was wrong because the surviving West children told social workers that Heather was buried under the patio.

Savage was able to get a search warrant in February 1994 and started digging in the garden. The excavation uncovered human bones.

The next day, Fred West surrendered to the police and confessed. Additional bodies were excavated at the house and Fred confessed to nine murders. Police were also able to locate two more victims near the village of Kempley. On June 30, 1994, Fred was charged with 11 murders and Rosemary with 10 murders.

Fred West escaped justice by hanging himself in his cell at a prison in Birmingham on New Year's Day, 1995. Before his death, Fred West reportedly told Janet Leach his "Appropriate Adult" or legal representative that he and Rosemary had killed as many as 20 people. This allegation has never been proven. Rosemary was convicted of all 10 murders and sentenced to life in October 1995.

Next door to a Church

Ironically, Fred and Rosemary West's hell on earth at 25 Cromwell St. was located next door to a Seventh Day Adventist Church. In October 1996, one year after Rosemary's conviction, the West family home was torn down by the local government. To discourage souvenir hunting, authorities crushed every brick from the home and burned all the wood.

Rosemary West is still in prison in England and maintains her innocence. She attracted some attention in 2003 when she became engaged to glam rocker Dave Glover, the bassist with Slade. Glover called off the engagement after being kicked out of the band.

Fred and Rosemary West were the subjects of an acclaimed 2011 British TV miniseries called Appropriate Adult, which is based on Janet Leach's experiences with West. In an intriguing coincidence, actor Dominic West (star of The Wire and The Hour) played Fred in the series. It isn't known if Dominic West is related to Fred West, but many people commented on the actor's similarity to Fred West when the program was broadcast.

THE MANSON GIRLS: HIPPIES TURNED KILLER GROUPIES

If any monster holds a special place in the American imagination, it has to be petty criminal turned hippy cult leader Charles Manson. He and his followers turned what was supposed to be an era of peace and love into a time of terror and mayhem.

The most horrifying thing about Manson was that he was able to turn three ordinary American college girls into vicious and sadistic killers. He did this by convincing them that horrific crimes, including murder, robbery, extortion, and torture, would trigger a revolution that would create a better world.

Three Average American Girls

Three of Charles Manson's most devoted and destructive followers were middle class girls. Their lives veered terribly off course during the counter-culture chaos of the 1960s, making them easy targets for the charismatic predator known as Charles Manson.

Susan Atkins (a.k.a. Sadie Mae Glutz) sang in a church choir as a girl. After her mother died, she dropped out of high school and moved to the hippy haven of San Francisco. Instead of participating in the summer of love, she worked as a topless dancer and a gun moll. She later became an LSD tripping flower child before joining Manson's "family".

Patricia Diane (or Big Patty) Krenwinkel grew up in an ordinary home in Los Angeles. Her father was an insurance salesman and her mother a homemaker. Incredibly, Krenwinkel was a devout Catholic who considered becoming a nun. She taught catechism to children and attended a Jesuit college in Alabama. She later dropped out, quit her job, and went on a school bus tour of the American West with Manson and the family.

Leslie Van Houten was a former homecoming queen with a checkered past. Reports indicate that she beat her adopted sister with a shoe. Van

Houten became pregnant and had an abortion when she was just 15. After leaving high school, Van Houten studied to be a legal secretary and tried LSD.

Van Houten joined the Manson family while traveling around California doing drugs. When she joined the family, Manson gave Van Houten to his right hand man, Charley "Tex" Watson, as a sex toy. Even though Manson ignored her, Van Houten was completely devoted to the madman and would do anything for him.

From Hippies to Killers

The girls became trapped in the darkest part of America's 1960s counter culture, the Manson family, which was a combination cult and commune that supposedly believed in free love and drugs. Manson masqueraded as a hippy guru, but he was really an ex-con and drifter with a long criminal record.

Unlike most hippies, Manson didn't believe in peace and love. Instead, he had a bizarre belief in what was called Helter Skelter, a violent race war that would destroy America. Manson later claimed that he ordered the murders to spark this bloodbath. By 1968, the family was dividing its time between two ranches in Death Valley and Spahn's Movie Ranch, an abandoned movie set near Los Angeles.

The Crime Spree

The family's crime spree began on May 18, 1969 when Manson apparently shot a drug dealer named Bernard Crowe at his Hollywood apartment. Manson told his followers he shot Crowe, who was African American, to start Helter Skelter. A more plausible motive for the crime is that Manson couldn't pay Crowe money he owed him.

Susan Atkins participated in the next murder on July 25, 1969. Manson sent Atkins and two other family members to extort money from a man named Gary Hinman. The three held Hinman hostage for two days. Atkins watched as Manson slashed Hinman's ear off with a sword. Another family member, Bobby Beausoleil, killed Hinman. Manson tried to blame the African American radical group, the Black Panthers, for the crime by painting one of their symbols on the wall. Manson told his followers he was trying to trigger a race war, but the real motive seems to have been $21,000 the family thought Hinman had.

Manson launched his Helter Skelter race war on Aug. 8, 1969 by sending Tex Watson, Atkins, Krenwinkel, and another woman, Linda Kasabian, to the former home of his acquaintance, Terry Melcher. The home was owned by a music executive named Ray Altobelli, who had been introduced to Manson by Beach Boy Dennis Wilson.

Manson knew that two well-known celebrities, movie director Roman Polanski and his wife Sharon Tate, were living in the home. Polanski was in London, but Tate was entertaining a number of friends, including hairstylist Jay Sebring, screenwriter Wojciech Fryowski, and Abigail Folger, heiress to the Folger's Coffee fortune.

The killing began when Tex Watson killed teenager Steve Parent, an innocent bystander in the home's driveway. Watson, Atkins, and Krenwinkel then went into the house and attacked Tate and her friends in the living room. Krenwinkel was particularly vicious; she fought with Folger, stabbed her, then chased the heiress outside. Once outside, Krenwinkel stabbed Folger again, then asked Watson to stab her as well. Krenwinkel was stabbing Tate, and the others, including Atkins, stabbed the pregnant Tate, Sebring, and Frykowski to death.

Atkins added a particularly horrific touch by writing the word PIG on the front door in Tate's blood. This touch was intended to make police and the media think that the Black Panthers, who called police pigs, and not the all-white family were responsible for the butchery.

The next night, Manson himself decided to participate in a slaughter. Family members Atkins, Krenwinkel, Watson, Ksabian, Van Houten, and Steve Clem joined him in a drive around town looking for victims. They eventually picked a wealthy grocer named Leno LaBianca, whom they apparently didn't know.

The family tied Leno and his wife up and told them it was a robbery. When Leno's wife, Rosemary, tried to fight back, Van Houten held her down while Krenwinkel stabbed her in the chest. Krenwinkel failed to complete the job, so Watson finished it. Watson then ordered Van Houten to stab Rosemary, and she stabbed the woman 14 times.

Capture and Celebrity

Ironically enough, it was a police investigation of one of the family's less violent activities, car theft, that led to their arrests. Police raided Spahn Ranch on Aug. 16, 1969 and arrested some family members for auto theft, but let them go. In October, sheriff's deputies raided Manson's other hideout at Barker Ranch in Death Valley and arrested the family again.

Once in custody, the so-called family quickly turned on each other. Another member of the family fingered Atkins for her involvement in the Hinman murder. Atkins told two jailhouse informants that she had participated in the Tate killing and even tasted Tate's blood. Police used this information to get warrants and round up the rest of the family.

Atkins showed her loyalty to Manson by testifying against the family to avoid the death penalty. Manson, Krenwinkel, Van Houten, and Atkins were tried and convicted of the Tate and LaBianca murders in 1970. The prosecution withdrew its offer to Atkins, who was sentenced to death, along with Krenwinkel, Manson, and Van Houten. Instead,

Kasabian, who had not taken part in the murders, testified against the family in exchange for immunity.

Atkins was convicted of Hinman's murder at a second trial held after the first one. At that trial, Atkins admitted the motive for the crime was robbery.

By the time of their trials, the Manson girls had become celebrities and the trials were something of a media circus. The publicity surrounding them made the family part of American pop culture.

Celebrities Behind Bars

Celebrity couldn't help the Manson girls avoid the death penalty; they were moved to California's newly-built Death Row for Women - which was never used because the California State Supreme Court declared the state's death penalty unconstitutional in 1972. Instead, all three girls and Manson were sentenced to life in prison.

In 1974, Susan Atkins claimed to become a born again Christian. In 1977, she wrote an autobiography called Child of Satan, Child of God, in which she contradicted some of her statements to the court. In 1981, Atkins married Donald Lee Laisure, a conman who claimed to be a multimillionaire. She ended the marriage in 1982 after finding out Laisure was broke. In 1987, Atkins married a Harvard trained lawyer named James W. Whitehouse. Atkins died in the Central California Women's Facility in 2009 of unknown causes. By then, she had made numerous parole requests, all of which had been denied.

Van Houten's attorneys were able to convince a judge to grant her a new trial in 1977. The grounds for this decision were that Van Houten's lawyer at the first trial, Ronald Hughes, had been killed before he could defend her. Van Houten's second trial ended in a hung jury; she was found guilty and sentenced to life in prison in a third trial.

Krenwinkel and Van Houten are still serving their life sentences in California state prisons. Both have been denied parole, but have managed to stay in the public spotlight by granting interviews. Krenwinkel is reportedly a model prisoner that earned a bachelor's degree behind bars. Krenwinkel and Van Houten are reportedly serving their time at the same prison, the California Institution for Women in Chino.

Doped Up Criminals

Despite its reputation as Satan-worshipping monsters, the Manson family was nothing but a criminal gang. The real motivation for their crime spree was apparently robbery to get money to buy drugs, not starting a race war. The most heinous thing about the Manson girls is that they allowed themselves to be manipulated by a psychopath. Worst of all, they became celebrities for killing innocent people.

THERESA KNORR: KID KILLER

Theresa Knorr was one of several female serial killers who preyed upon her own children. Theresa's crimes were particularly heinous because she tortured her own daughters for several years before brutally murdering them. To add insult to injury, Knorr forced three of her own daughters into prostitution.

Like Rosemary West and Gertrude Baniszewski, Knorr forced her other children to participate in her crimes. In one loathsome incident, she ordered her son to perform amateur surgery on his sister, an act that led to her death.

Insanity and the Death of a Husband

Theresa Knorr was born Theresa Cross in Sacramento, Calif. in 1946. Little is known about her childhood, but Theresa was deeply affected by the death of her mother in 1961.

Theresa Knorr married a man named Howard Clyde Sanders in 1964 when she was just 16. The two then moved to the small town of Galt, Calif., where Theresa apparently got away with Howard's murder. Theresa killed Sanders with a gunshot in the summer of 1964 when she was seven months pregnant with her second child, Sheila. Knorr was able to beat the rap by claiming self defense; judging by Theresa's history, it is safe to assume she killed Sanders in cold blood.

Theresa married Robert Knorr whom she had been having an affair with in 1966. She was seven months pregnant with Robert Knorr's child, Suesan Marlene Knorr, when she married.

Insanity and Abuse

The Knorr household was turned into a house of horrors by Theresa's insanity and sadism. Her children later told interviewers that she subjected all of them to intense levels of verbal, physical, and mental abuse.

The abuse was driven by a pathological hatred of Theresa's two daughters, Suesan Marlene Knorr and Sheila Sanders. Theresa reportedly thought both girls were witches that cast spells upon her.

The belief was that the girls cast spells upon Theresa to make her old and ugly.

The abuse went far beyond normal physical beatings. It had a sadistic edge to it that is completely frightening. Suesan was forced eat massive amounts of lard, which caused her to vomit. When Suesan vomited, Theresa forced her to eat the vomit. The girls were also beaten and burned with cigarettes.

If that wasn't bad enough, Theresa forced Sheila into prostitution in order to pay the family's bills. Theresa would cease the beatings as long as Sheila was bringing home cash.

Starving Her Own Daughter to Death

Not surprisingly, Sheila contracted venereal disease from one of her customers. Theresa punished Sheila for this by chaining her to the kitchen table. The mother did this because she was afraid the family would contract the venereal disease if Sheila used the toilet.

Knorr escalated her mistreatment of Sheila by hogtying her and locking her in the closet. Sheila was deprived of food and water and eventually died of starvation and dehydration. When Sheila died, Theresa had her son put the body in a box and dump it by the side of the highway. Shockingly, the body was never identified or linked to the Knorr family.

With Sheila unable to work, Theresa next forced Suesan into prostitution. Unlike Sheila, Suesan kept receiving beatings from Theresa, even though she was working.

One day in 1983, Knorr shot Suesan in a fit of anger. Instead of taking the girl to the hospital, Theresa chained Suesan to the bathtub and left her in the bathroom to die. Incredibly, Suesan survived and even recovered, even though she still had the bullet in her body.

Once Suesan had recovered, she told her mother she wanted to move out. Theresa gave her permission with the condition that the bullet lodged in Suesan's back be removed. Instead of going to the doctor, Theresa had her son, who had no medical training, cut the bullet out with a box cutter.

The result of such amateur surgery was predictable: Suesan's wound became infected. The girl became so sick that she collapsed into a coma. Instead of seeking medical help, Theresa Knorr left Suesan on the floor to die. Knorr made her children walk over Suesan.

Once Suesan died, Knorr and her sons, Robert and Bill, hauled Suesan's body to Truckee, Calif. in the mountains near Lake Tahoe. Once there, they poured gasoline over Suesan's body and set it on fire. Theresa took this action because she thought Suesan was possessed by a demon, and the only way the demon could be purged was with fire.

A Daughter's Escape Brings a Monster to Justice

Theresa's youngest daughter, Terry, realized that her only chance of survival was to get out. Surprisingly, Theresa agreed to let her daughter leave if Terry helped burn down the family home to cover up the evidence of her crimes. Terry went along with Theresa and helped with the arson.

After leaving home, Terry Knorr went to authorities several times and tried to turn in her mother. It wasn't until 1993 that police finally listened to her and arrested Theresa, Robert, and William.

Theresa Knorr pleaded guilty to murder, conspiracy to commit murder, murder with special circumstances, multiple murder, and murder by torture in November 1993. She made the plea to avoid the death penalty after she learned one of her sons was planning to testify against her in order to avoid prosecution. At least one of Knorr's sons received a three-year prison sentence for his role in the horrors.

Art Imitates Life

Theresa Knorr's crimes were so atrocious that they actually inspired a horror movie. The 2010 film The Afflicted (released as Another American Crime overseas) loosely follows the real events. It ends more dramatically with one of the daughters killing the mother and brothers. The real events, it seems, were too bizarre, even for Hollywood.

BRENDA ANN SPENCER: PIONEER SCHOOL SHOOTER

Sadly enough, school shootings have become commonplace in today's world. Yet school shootings committed by girls are rare. That's what makes the school shooting carried out in the late 1970s by Brenda Ann Spencer so unusual.

When Brenda turned a San Diego elementary school into a shooting gallery in 1979, there had been no prior incidents to inspire her. Yet despite the differences, Brenda's shooting spree bears some eerie similarities to later massacres such as the ones in Columbine, Colo. and Newtown, Conn.

Indeed, Brenda was very similar to more famed male shooters such as Kip Kinkel. Like them, she was a troubled loner who took her frustrations out with a gun. Yet the way she did it was rather more frightening – she used a scope-sighted rifle and picked her targets out with precision.

A Troubled Loner

Like many troubled teenagers, Brenda Ann Spencer was a loner. She was also gay, which further set her apart from her peers. Brenda was also interested in guns – her father had given her a rifle for her 16th birthday. Worse, he gave her 500 rounds of ammunition.

It was how she used the rifle that made Brenda sort of a sick pioneer. She decided to use it to shoot students at an elementary school in her hometown of San Diego. The reason she chose Grover Cleveland Elementary School for her shooting spree was a chilling one. It was a target of convenience, located across the street from her home. The school was a clear shot for the young lady with the rifle.

On Jan. 29, 1979, Brenda Ann Spencer started shooting at the students in the schoolyard from her own bedroom window. In other words, she became a sniper and terrorized innocent children she didn't know, possibly for thrills.

Easy Targets

Brenda opened fire as Principal Burton Wragg opened the gate to let children into the schoolyard. Several children were lined up, which made them easy targets for her.

Fortunately, none of the kids were killed, but many of them were psychologically scarred for life. Wragg was killed as he tried to help the children escape from the sniper fire. The school custodian, Mike Suchar, was also killed when he tried to pull Wragg out of the line of fire. Eight children and a San Diego police officer who also tried to help the children were injured.

The most chilling part of the shoot spree were the reasons that Spencer gave for it. She said the children made "easy targets" and that she hated Mondays.

She Talked to Journalists

Police soon arrived and surrounded Spencer's house. She barricaded herself inside and threatened to come out shooting. What happened next was even more bizarre – Spencer began talking with police negotiators and a reporter who managed to reach her.

Eventually, Spencer gave up and went willingly with police. The reign of terror was over, but unfortunately, it wouldn't be the last. Since 1979, America has seen many school shooting sprees, including one at another Cleveland Elementary School in Stockton, Calif. Even San Diego has suffered several notable school shootings.

The Motives are Unknown

The motives for Brenda Ann Spencer's shooting spree are unknown. The statements she made at the time of her arrest made no sense. Since then, Spencer has been diagnosed with epilepsy and depression and given drugs to treat those conditions in prison. Spencer has also claimed that she was sexually abused by her father. A dysfunctional family may have contributed to the tragedy shortly after her conviction. Brenda's father married a 17-year-old girl.

When she was arrested, Spencer tested positive for drugs. After her arrest, police found that her house was full of empty whiskey bottles. Interestingly enough, Spencer herself was not obviously drunk or high when taken into custody.

Brenda Ann Spencer was tried as an adult and convicted of two counts of murder. The court sentenced her to 25 years to life in the California state prison system. She has been up for parole several times, but parole has never been granted. In 2009, the parole board ruled that it will not hear her case again until 2019.

Brenda Ann Spencer will probably die in prison because of the parole board ruling. Spencer is currently serving time at California's Chino Institution for Women, where her fellow inmates include members of the Charles Manson family.

CHARLENE GALLEGO: ONE HALF OF A KILLER COUPLE

Most female serial killers operate completely alone. Such ladies start killing on their own and keep killing with little or no help. Not Charlene Gallego; she didn't start killing until she met a second generation psychopath named Gerald Gallego.

Once they linked up, the Gallegos went on a killing spree that terrorized three states. The spree was one of the most sadistic because the two picked victims at random and often kept their prey prisoner so they could use them as sex slaves.

From Good Family to Serial Killing

Charlene Gallego didn't seem like the kind of person who would turn to crime. She grew up in a good family in Arden Park, a nice suburb of Sacramento. Her father was a successful executive and Charlene was raised in affluence.

As a girl, Charlene seemed destined for success; she was a good student with a high IQ. Charlene was also a talented violinist who did well until she entered high school. In high school, Charlene started going wrong when she discovered drugs and sex. She went from good student to spoiled rich girl and rebel in short order.

Sexual adventures led Charlene to two failed marriages. Like many rebellious teenagers, Charlene Williams seemed destined to grow up to be just a loser. That is, until she fell in love with a small-time hoodlum named Gerald Gallego.

Second Generation Murderer

Gerald Gallego came from a very different background than Charlene's. Gerald's father, who was also named Gerald, had been the first man to die in the state of Mississippi's gas chamber in 1955. Like his son, the father was a killer who had murdered two police officers.

Gerald's mother was a prostitute, and there is evidence that her son worked as an errand boy for her pimps. Gerald lost no time in following in his father's footsteps; by 1977 Gerald had been arrested 23 times and spent much of his time in jail. Gerald had also been married five times before he met Charlene.

Despite his criminal background and family history, there was no evidence Gerald had been involved in murder before he got involved with Charlene. The two met at a dive bar in Sacramento, and Charlene immediately became attracted to Gerald and his plan to create disposable sex slaves. She also supported Gerald with her job as a supermarket cashier.

Disposable Sex Slaves

By September 11, 1978, Gerald and Charlene were ready to put their sick plan into action. The two drove around Sacramento in a 1973 Dodge van trolling for victims. Gerald drove the van while Charlene went hunting for the sex slaves. Charlene was two months pregnant at the time.

Charlene eventually lured teenage girls Kippi Vaught and Rhonda Scheffler out of a shopping mall and into the van. Charlene promised them that they would smoke marijuana; instead, Gerald was waiting with a loaded pistol. Once the girls were in the van, Gerald drove them deep into the Sierra Nevada Mountains. There Gerald raped and killed the girls.

After the murder, Charlene and Gerald went to Reno, Nevada, and got married. Even though Charlene's parents didn't approve of the marriage, they helped Gerald get a fake ID. The fake ID allowed the ex-con to get a good job driving a truck for a meat distributor. Disturbingly enough, Charlene stole her cousin's birth certificate to create the fake ID.

Kidnapping at the Fair

Gerald repaid his in-laws' hospitality by leaving his job and killing again. In June 1979 Charlene lured two teenagers, Brenda Judd and Sandra Colley, away from the Washoe County Fair by offering them a job distributing leaflets. Once again she lured the two into Gerald's van.

Gerald drove the girls into the mountains again but on the way stopped at a hardware store to buy a hammer and a shovel. After stopping for supplies, Charlene drove the van while Gerald assaulted the girls in the back. When the van stopped, Gerald used the hammer to kill the girls and the shovel to bury their bodies.

The next kidnapping occurred at a Tower Records store in Sacramento in 1980. There Charlene lured two 17-year-olds named Stacey Ann Redican and Karen Twiggs into the van with an offer of free drugs. Instead of drugs, the girls received sexual assault and a deadly whack from Gerald's hammer.

The Killing Continues

In June 1980 Gerald and Charlene decided to go on vacation to Oregon. Part of their vacation fun was to kidnap and murder a local girl named Linda Aguilar. Aguilar was 21 years old, and she was pregnant. Gerald killed her anyway by hitting her with a rock and strangling her.

Gerald's next target was Virginia Mochel who tended bar at the Sail Inn, one of his hangouts in West Sacramento. Gerald kidnapped Mochel, who had two children, after her shift, put her in the van, raped her, then murdered her and dumped her body in the countryside. This time Gerald had made a mistake; he had murdered somebody the police could connect him to. Cops looking into Mochel's disappearance were soon knocking at the Gallegos' door.

Even though Virginia Mochel's body was discovered, police couldn't connect the disappearance to Gerald Gallego, but they were suspicious. Gerald left town then came back and linked up with Charlene again. The two borrowed Charlene's parents' car, an Oldsmobile.

Kidnapping and Road Trip

Gerald and Charlene used the Oldsmobile to kidnap a young couple, Craig Miller and Mary Beth Sowers. This time they made another mistake; a friend of Miller's saw the kidnapping and wrote down the license plate number of the Oldsmobile.

Gerald drove Craig Miller into the countryside and shot him to death. He then took Mary Beth back to his apartment and raped her.

This time Gerald and Charlene would get caught; when they returned to Charlene's parents' house, the police were waiting for them. The two talked themselves out of the situation and fled town. First they drove to Reno, where they dumped the Oldsmobile and took the bus to Salt Lake City, Denver, and Omaha. Along the way, Charlene kept calling her parents for money.

It was the calls for money that led to the duo's capture. Charlene's parents agreed to wire money to the two at a Western Union office in Omaha. When they arrived to get the cash, the FBI was waiting for Charlene and Gerald. The two were arrested and extradited to California. By that time investigators had matched bullets from Gerald's gun to those in Craig Miller's body.

Two Generations on Death Row

Charlene Gallego eventually pleaded guilty to the murders of Craig Miller and Mary Beth Sowers. She then turned on Gerald Gallego and testified against him. Gerald doomed his future by serving as his own attorney. Charlene protected herself by testifying against Gerald Gallego in two states—California and Nevada.

Gerald followed in his father's footsteps by going to Nevada's death row. He cheated the executioner by succumbing to a far more painful death in 2002—cancer. Charlene Gallego is a free woman today; she was released from prison in 1997 and lives at an undisclosed location.

SARA ALDRETE: FROM GOOD STUDENT TO BLACK-MAGIC CULT KILLER

The story of Sara Aldrete, the Mexican cult killer known as La Madrina, resembles that of the women in the Manson family. Like the Manson women, Aldrete was a good student from a middle class family who was lured into Satanism, murder, and drug dealing by a small-time criminal turned cult leader.

Successful Student Meets the Godfather of Matamoros

Sara Maria Aldrete Villareal came from a middle class family in the city of Matamoros near the Texas-Mexico border. That alone gave Sara opportunities denied to most Mexican women. She was allowed to cross the border to study at Porter High School and later Texas Southwest High School in Brownsville, Texas.

At six foot one Sara stood out on campus; she was also a very good student who was planning to go on and study physical education. Sara's life took a turn for the dark side when she encountered a Svengali named Adolfo de Jesus Constanzo.

Constanzo was a small-time dope peddler, two-bit gang leader, and former fashion model with delusions of grandeur. Like Charles Manson, Constanzo had the ability to talk others into doing what he wanted. By the time he ran into Aldrete, Constanzo was running a small crew of drug dealers and styling himself "El Padrino de Matamoros" (The Godfather of Matamoros).

Dating a Drug Dealer

Sara met Constanzo when she was dating a rival drug dealer named Gilberto Sosa in 1987, whose operation Constanzo wanted to move in on. El Padrino introduced himself to Sara and charmed her into joining his cult. He introduced her to black magic, drug dealing, and other deviant activities.

Soon Sara was calling herself an expert in witchcraft, and the godmother of El Padrino's drug crew turned to sick religion. Even though El Padrino claimed to have spiritual powers, his real power came from the barrel of gun and his abilities as a con artist.

The religion Constanzo and Aldrete cooked up was extremely bizarre. Constanzo promised his followers superpowers, such as invulnerability and invisibility in exchange for 50% of their profits. Incredibly, he even convinced a local drug lord named Elio Hernandez to join his flock.

Human Sacrifice

At some point in 1988 El Padrino decided that human sacrifice was necessary for his "faith." In May 1988 Constanzo shot a drug dealer and a local farmer at his ranch near Matamoros. Then, in July 1989, the cult tortured a transvestite named Raul Paz Esquivel to death and dismembered his body in Mexico City.

Constanzo told his followers that the sacrifices were necessary to manipulate demons. He even told his followers that they must die screaming. Reports indicate that Sara Aldrete was an enthusiastic participant in the killings, cutting victims up with machetes and sometimes shooting them. At first the victims were rival drug dealers and other cult members, but Constanzo soon had his goons kidnapping people off the streets.

Someone Who Will Scream

El Padrino went too far in March 1989 when he ordered his followers to bring him someone who would scream for his next sacrifice. The followers dragged an innocent American student named Mark Kilroy off the streets. The kidnapping of an American caused police to start investigating.

The cops convinced a member of the Hernandez family to lead them to the ranch used as cult headquarters on April 9, 1989. There police found the remains of 15 victims but didn't find El Padrino. Having more faith in a fast car than magical powers, El Padrino and La Madrina had fled to Mexico City with some of their followers.

The family was hot; police on both sides of the border were looking for them. Geraldo Rivera even came to Matamoros and made a TV special about the killings. Rumors about Sara Aldrete also began to swirl. The most ridiculous was that she was planning to murder ten Anglo children in retaliation for the arrest of cult members. In Pharr, Texas, a church that was linked to El Padrino by rumors was burned by arsonists.

Hiding in Plain Sight

Constanzo and Aldrete were actually hiding in plain sight in an apartment house in Mexico City. The cult leader promised his followers that "they (authorities) cannot kill you." Yet he kept an Uzi machine pistol next to his bed for safety.

By then authorities were closing in; they had arrested another cult member named Jorge Montes, who told authorities everything about El Padrino's operation. Constanzo was further enraged by a TV news report that showed police supervising a Catholic exorcism on El Padrino's ranch.

Everybody in the cult, including Aldrete, began to fear for their lives as El Padrino became increasingly paranoid. Aldrete realized that the only way to survive was to try to contact the police by tossing a note out the window. A pedestrian found the note but thought it was a joke and ignored it.

Police Stumble on El Padrino

Ironically enough, the police found El Padrino and La Madrina by accident; officers searching for a missing child in another case stumbled on the apartment they were staying in. Police surrounded the apartment house, and a 45-minute gun battle ensued.

The magical powers didn't protect El Padrino, but they seemed to protect the police, who were not hurt by the cult's gunfire. Instead, realizing the game was up, Constanzo ordered one of his henchmen to shoot him. When the SWAT team entered the apartment, they found El Padrino dead and La Madrina very much alive.

The Godfather Didn't Rise from the Grave

Aldrete told police that "the godfather will not be dead for long" and would soon rise from the grave like Jesus Christ. When Constanzo stayed in the grave, Aldrete changed her story and claimed to be an innocent victim of his cult. Authorities didn't believe her story. She was sentenced to 62 years in prison and is still serving time in a Mexican prison.

Even if she gets out of the Mexican lockup, Aldrete will have answer to another higher power. U.S. prosecutors have stated they will charge Aldrete if she is ever released from a Mexican prison.

One mystery remains in the case of La Madrina and El Padrino. Nobody knows how many people they and their cult really killed. Investigators found 15 bodies at the ranch in Matamoros, and they have evidence of at least one murder in Mexico City. Observers believe there were more murders that went undetected. Current estimates indicate the cult is suspected in at least 16 other killings. El Padrino's drug crew might go down as one of the bloodiest cults in history.

LEONARDA CIANCIULLI: SHE MADE HER VICTIMS INTO SOAP

Leonarda Cianciulli has to be one of the strangest and most unlikely serial killers in history. The Italian woman looked like a grandmother yet she murdered three women and turned them into soap.

The so-called "Soap Maker of Corrgeggio"'s motive for murder was equally bizarre. She claimed to be performing human sacrifices designed to lift a curse off of her family and protect her son's life.

The most frightening aspect of Leonarda Cianciulli's personality was that she was known as a nice gentlewoman in the Neapolitan village of Correggio, where she lived. Leonarda even had a reputation as a doting mother and a good neighbor.

Yet she was driven by demons that turned her into a monster.

A Hard Life and a Superstitious Woman

Leonarda Cianciulli had lived a very hard life. She was raised in poverty in one of the poorest regions of Italy. Her plight was worsened because she married a man her parents didn't approve of. Leonarda later claimed her mother put a curse on her that caused her problems.

Later on Leonarda served time in prison for fraud, lost three sons in childbirth, and saw her house burn down in an earthquake. Being a very superstitious woman, she blamed these problems on the evil curse rather than bad luck.

Times were bad in Italy and getting worse. Fascist dictator Benito Mussolini was preparing to follow his "friend" Adolph Hitler into World War II, a conflict that average Italians knew Italy could not win. Mussolini started drafting Italian men, including Cianciulli's son Giuseppe, as part of the buildup to the war.

Draft Notice Leads to Bizarre Serial Killing

It was Giuseppe's draft notice that triggered the killing of three women. Leonarda was afraid that her son would be killed in the war. So like a good mother, she took steps to protect him in uniform; the steps involved human sacrifice and soap making.

The first victim was Faustina Setti, an unmarried woman who sought out Leonarda's services as a matchmaker. Leonarda claimed that she could find a suitable mate for Faustina in the town of Pola in exchange for the woman's life savings. Instead of arranging a marriage, Leonarda knocked Setti out with a glass of drugged wine, cut up her body, and boiled it down for soap.

Cianciulli lured in her next victim, Francesca Soavi, with a false job offer. After taking Soavi's money, Leonarda drugged her, killed her with an axe, and boiled her body down for soap.

Leonarda had also invented a method of fooling her victims' friends and families; she talked them into writing postcards and mailed them. This made the friends and family think the victims were still alive. The failure of this ruse led to Cianciulli's detection.

Making the Soprano into Soap

On September 30, 1940, Leonarda Cianciulli succeeded in luring her third victim, Virginia Cacioppo, to her house with a false job offer. Cacioppo, a former opera singer, was very well off; she reportedly had 50,000 lire in jewels and cash in her possession.

Like the other two, Cacioppo was drugged, cut up, and boiled down for soap. This time Cianciulli added another disturbing twist; she added cologne to the soap. To add to the horror, Leonarda gave bars of the soap to her friends and neighbors as presents.

Virginia Cacioppo's sister-in-law began wondering about her disappearance and started investigating. When she learned her sister-in-law had last been seen entering a business Cianciulli owned in Correggio, the sister-in-law told the police. Police investigated and soon discovered enough evidence to arrest Leonarda.

Trial and a Long Life in the Asylum

Leonarda Cianciulli wasn't tried for murder until 1946 because of World War II. Such events as the Allied invasion of Italy, Nazi occupation, and Mussolini's downfall made it hard to try her.

At her trial in 1946 Cianciulli admitted what she had done and made the bizarre claims about human sacrifice to protect her son. Whether she believed it or if it was simply a ruse to cover up murder for money is not known. Leonarda was sentenced to 30 years in a woman's criminal asylum, where she died in 1970.

If you want to see Leonarda's soap cooking pot, it is on display at the Italian Criminological Museum in Rome. Her case still attracts interest and thrills tourists over 40 years after her death.

MAGDALENA SOLIS: THE HIGH PRIESTESS OF BLOOD

The story of Mexico's Magdalena Solis is almost too incredible to believe. The serial killer and leader of a blood drinking sex cult sounds like something out of a B movie, yet she was real.

Solis grew up in a poor dysfunctional family in the Mexican state of Monterrey in the 1940s and 1950s. Her early life was obscure and there was little noticeable about her. Like Charles Manson, she was a small-time criminal who turned into a monster when she got involved in a cult. Unlike Manson, Solis took over somebody else's cult rather than forming her own.

Before she became a cult leader, Solis was apparently a local prostitute. Her pimp was her brother Eleazar, another local criminal.

Petty Scam turns into Killer Cult

Ironically enough, Magdalena Solis's sex and murder cult started as a scam created by two small-time conmen. In 1962, a pair of traveling charlatans named Santos and Cayentano Hernandez wandered into the dusty town of Yerba Buena, Monterey. The two hucksters decided to try their latest scam, the Inca God cult, on the yokels.

The scamming brothers claimed to be high priests of the "exiled Inca Gods." In exchange for offerings, the Inca Gods would reveal the location of a buried treasure to the true believers. The scam seemed to work well and the collection plates of the Hernandez brothers were soon full. There was one problem – the two recruited Magdalena Solis as their accomplice.

When the suckers started asking where the treasure was, the brothers fooled them with a new scam. They used a cheap magic trick to try and pass off Solis as the reincarnation of a goddess. The idea was that the gullible would give more donations to the goddess. The only problem was that the power of being a goddess quickly went to Magdalena's head.

The Goddess and the Blood Ritual

Instead of continuing to work the scam, Solis took over the cult and began adding her own touches. The goddess began claiming that the Gods were not happy with revealing the location of the treasures because they weren't getting any human sacrifices.

The sacrifices took the form of rituals based on bloody Aztec practices suppressed by the Spanish conquistadores. Solis's followers lured two prostitutes to Yerba Buena and killed them. Like Charles Manson, Solis was smart enough to have her followers take part in the murders. They beat, burned, and mauled the victims to death.

Solis then added another touch. She ordered blood drained from the victims. Her followers then had to drink the blood in a sick mockery of the Catholic Mass. Not surprisingly, the high priestess of blood began demanding more and more sacrifices. At least four people were lured to Yerba Buena and sacrificed to the goddess.

Using Sex to Control her Followers

Solis used another tactic to control her followers that Charles Manson later adopted. She convinced them to take part in orgies and deviant sexual practices. This made the activity fun and set the followers apart from respectable society.

By this time, in 1963, the cult's activities were well organized. The followers even had a sort of temple set up in a cave, and their ceremonies were beginning to attract attention. Unfortunately, what was going on was just too fantastic for most people to believe.

Too Fantastic for the Police to Believe

The police were first alerted to the high priestess of blood and her activities by a 14-year-old boy named Sebastian Guerrero, who wandered by the cave where the sacrifices were going on and took a look. Sebastian was so horrified by the activities that he ran 25 kilometers to the nearest police station to alert the authorities.

Guerrero told the cops that he had seen vampires at work and the police naturally didn't believe him. Yet one officer, Investigator Luis Martinez, decided there might be something to the story and accompanied Guerrero to take a look at the cave.

This led to Solis's arrest and the end of the cult because neither Guerrero nor Martinez came back from the cave. Authorities could ignore the ramblings of a 14-year-old boy, but they couldn't ignore a missing police officer. They decided to search the town of Yerba Buena and find out what was really going on there.

The Army Gets Called In

When the authorities finally moved in on Yerba Buena on May 31, 1963, they took no chances. This time, police called in the Army for help. Soldiers and cops fanned out through the town and started rounding up what they called Satanists. The power of the Inca Gods was no match for the firepower of the military.

During the roundup, Santos Hernandez was shot by the police and Cayentano Hernandez was killed by one of his own followers. Magdalena Solis and her brother Elezar were arrested at a nearby farm. Unlike the Hernandez brothers, the goddess and her brother put up no fight.

Investigators searched the town and found the bodies of Sebastian Guerrero and Luis Martinez near the caves. The bodies had been dismembered, as had several other bodies in the caves. Police also found a large stash of marijuana in the Solis house, which indicates the goddess used drugs and sex to control her followers like Manson later would.

Magdalena and Eleazar Solis were sentenced to 50 years in prison for the killings of Guerrero and Martinez. They were never charged with the other murders, although police believe they may have killed at least six other people. If Magdalena Solis is still alive, she should be released sometime in 2013, the 50th anniversary of her arrest.

Did She Inspire Charles Manson?

An intriguing question about Magdalena Solis is her possible influence on Charles Manson, a small-time criminal who was serving prison time in Washington State at the time of Solis's activities. It is possible that Manson may have been inspired by newspaper accounts of the high priestess of blood and used them as a basis for his bloody family. After all, Manson's rampage in Los Angeles in 1969 took place just a few years after Solis's arrest.

MARTHA BECK: THE LONELY HEARTS KILLER

It was a bizarre prank played by a coworker that changed Martha Beck from a successful, if overweight, nurse into a serial killer. In the late 1940s Martha Beck was a successful nurse working in Pensacola, Florida; she was also a very lonely woman because her obesity (she weighed 250 pounds) repelled most men.

At some point a coworker sent Beck an advertisement for something called Mother Dinene's Family Club for Lonely Hearts, a 1940s equivalent of Internet dating services, basically a catalog of eligible singles. Beck, who was single, put in an ad to see if she could find a man.

The man she found was a vicious serial killer named Raymond Fernandez, and she decided to join his killing spree. Fernandez was a former merchant marine sailor who had begun preying on women he met through lonely hearts clubs. Fernandez was also obsessed with the occult and even practiced voodoo. The two quickly became the most notorious serial killers of 1940s America.

A Lonely and Overweight Sex Addict

Martha Beck was a lonely and troubled woman; she was severely overweight, but she was also a sex addict. During World War II she had been a so-called V-girl who had sex with servicemen before they left for duty. After the war she got pregnant and married a man she didn't love. Eventually she ended up living a lonely existence, spending most of her time reading trashy romance pulp magazines.

Despite her problems, Beck was also a very successful nurse who earned a good living. She had completed college, and her superiors approved of the work she did. Martha Beck was also a devoted mother with two young children. Yet she gave that all up for Raymond Fernandez.

In 1947 Beck and Fernandez began corresponding. By that time Fernandez had ripped off dozens of lonely women and murdered at least one of them. Fernandez wrote back to Beck because he figured she had a good job and money he could steal.

Dream Man Turns out to Be a Monster

In December 1947 Martha Beck's dream man, Raymond Fernandez, arrived in Pensacola, Florida, from New York City. After meeting Beck and discovering she had no money, he went back to New York. Beck decided to follow Fernandez to New York, and that's when her life took a turn to the dark side.

The first thing Beck did in New York was to abandon her own children by dumping them at the Salvation Army. Beck didn't see her own kids again until she was on death row at Sing Sing Prison a few years later. The next thing she did was to move in with Fernandez.

Once they moved in together, Fernandez explained how he made his living to her. He travelled around the United States ripping off women he met through the lonely hearts ads. Martha decided to join Raymond in this horrendous activity and take it even further.

Love and Murder

For several months Fernandez married one woman after another and stole their money. He introduced Martha to his lovers as his sister. The racket worked until August 1948.

In that month Raymond Fernandez married a woman named Myrtle Young from Arkansas. Myrtle soon complained about Fernandez's living arrangements; she had to sleep in the same bed as

Martha. When her complaints got vocal, Fernandez administered Myrtle a fatal dose of drugs and put her on the bus. He and Martha also helped themselves to $4,000 that Myrtle was carrying. Myrtle died in a hospital in Little Rock, Arkansas, after being unconscious on the bus.

The next victim was Janet Fay of Albany, New York, a 66-year-old widow. In January 1949 Janet married Raymond Fernandez, then took $6,000 out of her bank accounts. Once they had the money, Martha and Fernandez killed Fay and stuffed her body in a trunk. They first stored the trunk in Raymond's sister's basement, then buried it in the basement of a house.

Killing a Mother and Her Baby

The next crime was a particularly horrendous one. Raymond Fernandez's next victim was Delphine Downing of Grand Rapids, Michigan, a widow who had a two-year-old daughter. Downing thought that Fernandez was a successful businessman named Charles Martin.

Shortly after Janet Fay's death, Charles Martin turned up in Grand Rapids. Delphine was confused because Martin had brought his "sister" Martha with him. Yet she still fell in love with the man. The love affair ended when Delphine saw Martin without his toupee; Raymond Fernandez was bald and had a terrible scar from a World War II injury on his head. Delphine accused Raymond of fraud and deception.

To calm her down, Martha and Raymond tricked Delphine into taking sleeping pills, which knocked her unconscious. This caused Delphine's two-year-old daughter Rainelle to start crying. The crying angered Martha, who choked Rainelle to death.

Once Rainelle was dead, Martha and Raymond realized that Delphine would call the police when she woke up. They didn't give her the chance; Raymond shot Delphine in the head with her own gun. The two then cleaned all the valuables out of the Downing house. They buried Delphine and Rainelle Downing in their own basement. After the murder, the Lonely Hearts Killers went to the movies.

Love and the Electric Chair on Death Row

The trip to the movies proved to be Fernandez and Beck's undoing; had they left town right away they might have escaped. Delphine Downing's neighbors, suspicious of what was happening, called the police. Officers investigated and tracked the two killers to the apartment where they had been staying.

The police took the killers to the local district attorney's office, where Raymond Fernandez immediately said, "I'm no average killer." The two then confessed all of their crimes, probably because Michigan had no death penalty at the time.

They felt confession was the way to avoid execution. Beck even believed that she might get out in less than six years for good behavior.

The ruse didn't work; instead of trying Fernandez and Beck, Michigan prosecutors extradited them to New York, which had the death penalty. The two were put on trial in the Bronx for Janet Fay's murder, where the tabloid press had a field day. Reporters labeled the two the Lonely Hearts Killers and Martha "Big Martha." Fernandez tried to claim he was innocent and blamed Beck for Fay's death. The jury didn't buy his arguments and sentenced both to death.

Raymond Fernandez and Martha ultimately shared the same fate. They were imprisoned on the same death row at New York's Sing Sing prison and died in the electric chair on March 8, 1951. Shortly before electrocution both Martha and Raymond professed their love for each other. The lonely hearts killers stayed together to the bitter end.

CHRISTINA MARIE RIGGS: SHE KILLED HER OWN CHILDREN

There is nothing more frightening or more heinous than a mother that kills her own children. Not
only is the crime unnatural, it is downright frightening. One of the most terrifying examples of such a
monster was Christina Marie Riggs, the first woman
executed in Arkansas since before the Civil War.
Riggs' crime was even more bothersome because
she was a nurse, a member of a profession dedicated to saving and preserving life.

From Working Mom to Murderer

In 1997 Christina Riggs seemed to have put a troubled life behind her and established a successful work and personal life. As a girl in Arkansas, Riggs claimed she was sexually abused by her own stepmother and a neighbor.

By the time she was 16, Riggs was drinking alcohol and smoking marijuana. She was also sexually promiscuous because she thought that was the only way to get boys. Riggs became pregnant, had a baby, and gave it up for adoption at age 16. Yet she managed to put those problems behind her and become a licensed practical nurse. Riggs even found a good job working at the Veterans Administration.

Even though her professional life was working out, her personal life wasn't. Her marriage to an Air Force enlisted man named Timothy Thompson produced two children but didn't work out. Thompson didn't seem to care about her or the children, and the relationship fell apart.

Did the Oklahoma City Bombing Ruin Her Life?

Riggs' life began to spin out of control after white supremacist and domestic terrorist Timothy McVeigh blew up the Murray Federal Building in her hometown of Oklahoma City. Riggs claims she was recruited to work triage, a stressful medical procedure in which medical professionals have to decide which wounded to treat, after the bombing. Prosecutors later claimed this was a lie.

What is known is that sometime after the bombing Riggs moved to Sherwood, Arkansas, and found work at the Arkansas Heart Hospital. She also worked through a nursing temporary agency. During this period Riggs began having money troubles.

Riggs became depressed at this time and found an answer to her troubles. She would kill herself and her two children, five-year-old son Justin and two-year-old daughter Shelby Alexis. The motives for this are unclear, but money troubles and loneliness may have exasperated existing mental problems.

Poisoning and Smothering the Little Ones

Christina Riggs decided to end her problem in November 1997. Her weapon of choice was poison, but like many poisoners, she underestimated how much poison it takes to kill a human being, even a small child. Riggs first gave the little ones an antidepressant drug, Elavil, which she thought would sedate them.

She then injected them with potassium chloride, a drug used in lethal injections and in open heart surgery. Unfortunately, she didn't give Justin and Shelby the proper dose. Instead of killing the children, the drug simply put them in agonizing pain. Realizing that she had botched the poisoning,

Riggs finished the job by smothering the little ones with a pillow. Since Riggs weighed 280 pounds, the small children didn't stand a chance.

After botching the murder, Riggs botched her own suicide. She took 28 tablets of Elavil and injected herself with potassium chloride. Riggs knocked herself out, but she survived because her mother, fearing for her grandchildren's lives, called the police. Two officers came to Riggs' home and found her unconscious. Riggs was rushed to a hospital, where doctors saved her life.

She Wanted to Die, Then She Didn't

Christina Marie Riggs was arrested by police immediately after she left the hospital. She went to trial in June 1998 and immediately became a symbol of controversy. Riggs pleaded guilty and claimed she had a medical defect. She also claimed that the murder of her children was "an act of love."

The prosecution claimed that Riggs had killed her children because they were limiting her social life. Prosecutors noted that the killing was planned and that Riggs preferred going to karaoke bars rather than spending time with her kids. The jury believed prosecutors and took just 55 minutes to sentence Riggs to death.

Riggs at first welcomed the death penalty, perhaps believing it would give her release. Yet she then filed some appeals and won some support from anti-death penalty groups.

The opposition didn't help; on May 2, 2000, Christiana Marie Riggs became the first woman to be put to death on Arkansas's death row. No other woman had been executed in the state since 1845. Her means of execution was an ironic one; she was killed by lethal injection, which uses a fatal mix of drugs that included potassium chloride to cause death. Riggs finally succeeded in killing herself by potassium chloride.

BETTY NEUMAR: SHE MURDERED FIVE HUSBANDS AND GOT AWAY WITH IT

Betty Neumar didn't fit the popular image of a black widow. Yet the tough country girl may have gotten away with marrying and possibly murdering five different husbands. The worst part of it was that her murder spree lasted nearly 40 years.

Authorities didn't become aware of Neumar's activities until 2008, but evidence indicates Neumar was killing husbands as early as 1955. Unfortunately, authorities seem to have unwittingly helped her cover up her crimes. The most disturbing part of Betty Neumar's murder spree is that her crimes were actually very blatant.

The Girl from Ironton

Betty Neumar grew up in Depression era poverty in the town of Ironton, Ohio, during the 1930s and 1940s. Like many women, she escaped poverty by marrying but found herself in another kind of trap.

Neumar's first husband was a man named Clarence Malone. The marriage didn't work out, but Malone gave Betty a son named Gary. Even though Clarence Malone divorced Betty, he may not have gotten away. In 1970 Malone was shot to death under mysterious circumstances outside his auto body shop in Northern Ohio. Police ruled his death a homicide but could find no suspects. It is unclear if Betty killed Malone or not.

Betty's second husband was a man named James Flynn, who disappeared in the mid-1950s. Neumar claimed that Flynn had died on a pier in New York City; unfortunately, no proof could be found of this. Nobody knows if James Flynn died or simply walked away. His body and proof of his death has never been found. Nor is there any proof that Flynn really existed or not.

A Suspicious Suicide

Betty Flynn, as she then called herself, resurfaced in Florida in the mid 1960s; by then she was married to a member of the Navy named Richard

Sillis. Sillis was found dead in his mobile home in Big Coppit, Florida, in 1967. Police ruled the case a suicide, believing that he had shot himself. Sillis's son has been trying to get authorities to reopen the case, claiming that Betty murdered his father.

No autopsy was ever performed on Richard Sillis, but a Navy medical examiner found that Sillis may have been shot twice. Plans to exhume Sillis's body for a new autopsy in 2009 were cancelled because of a weird technicality in Florida law.

There was no doubt about the death of Betty's fourth husband, Thomas Harold Gentry. He was shot several times in the couple's home in Norwood, North Carolina. Incredibly, Betty was never arrested for that crime and was allowed to marry again.

Poison and Final Capture

It took the death of Betty's fifth husband, John Neumar Sr., in 2007 to get police to start looking seriously at her marital habits. Neumar died of symptoms that indicated arsenic poison.

It was Neumar's son, John Jr., who tipped off authorities. John was angry because he learned of his father's death in the newspaper, not from his stepmother. John got suspicious when he heard that Betty had John Neumar Sr. cremated, which was clearly against the man's wishes. John Neumar had paid for a burial plot before his death. The cremation was probably ordered to cover up evidence of poison.

Police investigated and took a close look at Thomas Gentry's death in 1986. The local sheriff's office concluded that Betty had hired a hit man to kill Thomas Gentry. The motive for the killing was apparently a $20,000 life insurance policy Betty had taken out on Thomas.

Arrested but Never Tried

Betty Neumar was arrested and charged with Thomas Gentry's murder but never tried for the crime. Authorities arrested her after locating a former police officer whom she had allegedly hired to kill her husband.

Betty walked out of jail on $300,000 bond in October 2008 and died a free woman. She wasn't tried because changes in the local prosecutor's office kept postponing the trial. She was even allowed to travel to Louisiana.

Intriguingly, Betty Neumar's death was mysterious. Police announced that they would look into the mysterious illness that had killed her. Some reports indicate that Neumar died of cancer; others claim that no cause of death was listed. Authorities didn't say why they thought Betty Neumar's death was suspicious. The Black Widow may have been able to evade the law, but somebody may have taken the law into their own hands.

Nothing remains solved in the mystery of Betty Neumar; her cause of death is unknown, the mystery of James Flynn has never been solved, and the investigations into her husbands' deaths are closed. Unlike most black widows, Betty Neumar appears to have gotten away with murder.

JEANNE WEBER: THE FATAL BABYSITTER

The scariest female serial killers are those who target the most defenseless victims of all – children. An even scarier aspect to such killers is that some of them work as babysitters.

One of the worst was Jeanne Weber, a French-woman who killed her own children and those of her friends. Known as "The Ogress", Jeanne got away with murdering children for years before she was caught. Nobody knows how many children Jeanne killed, but the best estimates are around 10.

From Peasant Woman to Terror of Paris

Jeanne Weber lived a fairly typical life for a Frenchwoman in the early 1900s. She was born and raised in a poor village that she left for Paris at age 14. Once there, she married and worked at menial jobs, such as a maid. Her situation was made worse by the fact that her husband was an alcoholic who couldn't support the family.

Weber's first victim was her own niece, the daughter of her sister-in-law. On March 2, 1905, Weber's sister-in-law made the fatal mistake of asking her to babysit. One of the girls, 18-month-old Georgette, died while Weber was taking care of her. A doctor examined the body, but determined the death was by natural causes, even though there were bruises on the body.

Less than a month later, Weber came to babysit again on March 25, and Georgette's sister, seven-year-old Germaine, died. Four days later, Weber's own seven-year-old son died. Obvious strangulation marks on the children were again ignored.

Trying to kill her own nephew

Incredibly, the sisters-in-law again made the mistake of allowing Jeanne Weber to care for a child on April 5, 1905. On that day, they went out shopping and left 10-year-old Maurice with Jeanne. When the sisters returned, they found Maurice on his bed with bruises on his neck. Jeanne was standing over the boy with a crazed look on her face.

This time, Jeanne was arrested and put on trial for eight murders, three of which were of her own children. She was also accused of killing two other children. Unfortunately, a brilliant defense attorney named Henri-Robert took the case and was able to get Jeanne declared not guilty.

During the trial, prosecutors made the chilling accusation that Jeanne had killed her own son in an attempt to cover up the other murders she had committed. Despite this testimony, the court let a monster loose to kill again.

The Killing Continues

After the trial, Jeanne Weber dropped out of sight and left Paris. She turned up two years later in the French town of Villedieu. Her presence was discovered when nine-year-old Auguste Bavouzet was found dead with mysterious marks on his neck. A doctor that examined the body recognized a mysterious babysitter in the boy's house as Jeanne Weber.

Once again, Weber was arrested and got away with Henri-Robert's help. It was at this time that Jeanne started using assumed names to get closer to killing children.

Weber found work in places full of potential victims, including a children's hospital where she worked as an orderly. Then in an orphanage, she was fired after four days when she was caught trying to strangle a child. Police were not told, and

Weber was quietly fired to protect the home's reputation.

Prostitution and Capture

By 1908, Weber was back in Paris and working as a prostitute. She was also arrested for vagrancy and briefly confined to a mental institution. Finally, in the town of Commercy, France, an innkeeper caught Jeanne trying to strangle his son. The father was too late – the boy was already dead, but he had to punch Weber three times to get her to release the body.

This time, there was no escape for Jeanne Weber; she was bound over for trial, but declared insane. Instead of going to the guillotine, Jeanne Weber was sent to an insane asylum. There, the Ogress did to herself what she had done to her victims – she strangled herself to death.

Celebrity Serial Killer

Interestingly enough, Jeanne Weber was something of a celebrity during her lifetime. Her activities were widely reported in the French, American, and British press. Sensational articles described the Ogress's activities in the tabloid, even as she was killing children.

Observers blamed the authorities' inability to keep Jeanne Weber off the streets and the jurors' inability to believe that a woman would kill children. Such horrors, which are all too common to us today, were unthinkable in the early 20th century.

ENRIQUETA MARTÍ: THE MURDEROUS WITCH

The evilest and foulest female serial killer of all was Enriqueta Martí, the vampire of Barcelona. Martí was so depraved that she kidnapped children and sold them to men to use as sex slaves. Then to further exploit the children, she killed them and used parts of their bodies in "medicine" that she sold to her neighbors.

In addition to being a serial killer who was called a vampire by the press, Martí was also regarded as a witch by her neighbors. As a witch, she was able to sell salves, ointments, and other quack cures to them. The only problem was that many of the quack cures contained parts of the dead children's bodies.

Country Girl in the Big City

Enriqueta Martí was a country girl who moved to the big city of Barcelona in the 1890s. After an unsuccessful marriage to a painter, Martí became a prostitute, then decided that there was more money in running a brothel. She also decided that there was more money in running a very special and evil kind of brothel, one that specialized in providing children to pedophiles.

In 1909, Martí began kidnapping children off the streets of Barcelona and putting them to work in her brothel. The children came from the city's poorest families, while Martí's customers came from the upper classes. Testimony indicated that Martí went to the city's swankest night spots in order to recruit rich men as customers.

To cover up her activities, Martí murdered the children and used some of their bones and blood in her magic. Martí made skin cream out of the remains, which was sold to women in high society, in addition to the quack cures she peddled to the poor.

Authorities Cover-up for the Vampire

The worst part of Enriqueta Martí's activities was that authorities apparently covered up for her. Even though rumors about missing children were spreading on the streets, nobody seemed to care that poor children were disappearing. The mayor of Barcelona even told the newspapers that there were no missing children when there obviously were. He also claimed that children were not being kidnapped.

During the early 1900s, Spain's rich didn't care about all the poor peasants who were moving to the nation's big cities from the countryside. Instead, they viewed the peasants as a nuisance or a resource to be exploited, a situation that Enriqueta Martí took advantage of for profit.

Apartments of Horror

The mayor's claims were disproved in 1912 when one of Martí's neighbors noticed that a seven-year-old girl was trapped in her apartment. The woman called the police, who rescued the girl and found pieces of 10 different bodies in the apartment.

Worse horrors were to come when it was found that Martí had several apartments in different parts of Barcelona. Some of them were used as killing grounds for children. Another luxury apartment was used as the brothel, and some apartments were used to imprison kidnapped kids.

The horrors inflicted on the kidnapped children were especially grotesque. Martí forced the kids to call her "mom." Yet she didn't treat the children like a mother – she beat them and fed them stale bread and potatoes. Martí also beat the children if they didn't cooperate with her. When police searched the homes and apartments that Martí used, they found secret compartments full of bodies and body parts.

The Extent of the Horror is Unknown

There are many unanswered questions about Enriqueta Martí, with a big one being how she kidnapped the children. Reports indicate that she lured them off the streets with promises of candy, but these rumors have never been confirmed.

Another question is the number of victims – police found evidence of more than 10 victims, but there were probably more. Since Martí operated for several years and destroyed the victims' bodies, she may have murdered dozens of children. Her operation was also very elaborate and well-financed.

Mystery Remains to this Day

No evidence of accomplices was ever found, yet circumstantial evidence indicates somebody else must have known. Martí had a very elaborate and well-financed operation. Many poor people in Barcelona suspected that police or authorities were helping or protecting Martí.

No effort to punish the wealthy people who purchased the creams made from the children's body parts was made, nor was there any effort to punish the rich pedophiles that used her services. A reason for this may have been that authorities feared that news of the true extent of the horrors would have led to rioting and social upheaval. Barcelona had been rocked by deadly riots in 1909, in which churches were burned and workers were killed by troops.

The mystery is deepened by the fact that Enriqueta Martí was never tried for her crimes. Instead, she died in prison under mysterious circumstances in 1913. Officially, Martí died of a long illness, but she may have been murdered. Before her death, Martí admitted many of her crimes and started naming some of her customers. One of them may have arranged her death to keep the Vampire of Barcelona quiet.

Even in today's depraved age, Enriqueta Martí's crimes stand out. In the past 100 years, nobody seems to have matched the Vampire of Barcelona's record for evil and depravity.

LYNN TURNER: THE ANTIFREEZE KILLER

Poisoning a husband or a lover for the insurance money seems like an old-fashioned crime, but Black Widows still practice it. The stakes in such crimes are much higher because insurance payouts are much bigger. Yet the chance of getting caught is far higher because of modern forensics.

Atlanta 911 operator Lynn Turner learned this the hard way when she went to prison for poisoning a husband and boyfriend. Chillingly, one of the men she poisoned was the father of her two children.

To students of crime, Lynn Turner's case sounds a lot like classic 19th century poisoners, such as the black widows of Liverpool. Like them, she killed men for the insurance money and turned an ordinary item found in almost every household on Earth, antifreeze, into a deadly poison. The black widows of Liverpool boiled down flypaper to extract arsenic for their crimes.

Married to a Police Officer

In 1995 Lynn Turner seemed like an ordinary middle class woman living in Cobb County, Georgia. She even had a job with the purpose of saving lives; as a 911 dispatcher, she made sure help reached people in trouble. Turner was also married to a police officer named Maurice Glenn Turner.

Yet Turner had a dark side that came to the surface in that year. She began visiting a local animal shelter to play with abandoned cats. At the shelter, Turner learned that antifreeze can kill cats and dogs. The antifreeze commonly used in vehicles contains a poison named ethylene glycol, which is deadly when consumed in large amounts.

Lynn Turner, then known as Julia Lynn Womack, was still engaged to Maurice Turner when she approached insurance agent Vince Turley in 1993. The reason was to make Lynn the beneficiary of Maurice's life insurance policy. Lynn wouldn't even marry Maurice until she was sure her name was on his insurance policy.

She Gets Away with It Once

The worst thing about Lynn Turner is that she got away with murder once despite blatantly suspicious behavior. On March 2, 1995, Maurice Turner came to the emergency room because of convulsions and other symptoms. Incredibly, the doctor on duty, Donald Freeman, diagnosed Turner with ethylene glycol poisoning. Unfortunately, Freeman sent Officer Turner home.

Maurice Turner died the next day, but no autopsy was performed, so Lynn got away with it. She collected the $110,000 life insurance policy and promptly moved in with another man, Randy Thompson.

Even Lynn's own mother admitted on the stand that her daughter had acted "cold" at Maurice's funeral. It was obvious that Lynn Turner viewed men as sources of money rather than human beings.

She Kills the Father of Her Children

After Maurice's death Lynn lived with a firefighter named Randy Thompson for several years. She never married Thompson, but he did father her two children and made the terrible mistake of listing Lynn Turner as the beneficiary of his life insurance.

On January 22, 2001, Randy Thompson was found dead in his apartment in Cumming, Georgia. The death was viewed as suspicious because

Thompson was just 32 and capable of passing the physical exam to be a firefighter. Police asked the Georgia Bureau of Investigation to look into the case. The bureau first found that Thompson had died from an irregular heartbeat, then that the irregular heartbeat was caused by ethylene glycol poisoning.

Once authorities were aware of the cause of Randy Thompson's death, they ordered Maurice Turner's body exhumed for an autopsy. On October 21, 2001, the Cobb County Medical Examiner announced that Maurice Turner had died of ethylene glycol poisoning.

Even though police knew that Randy Thompson had been poisoned over a year earlier, Lynn Turner was not arrested and charged until November 1, 2002. It seems likely that detectives kept the true nature of Thompson's death secret in order to build a case against her. They may have been afraid that she would use the insurance money to finance a trip to a country without an extradition treaty with the United States.

Two Murder Trials

It's easy to see why investigators spent so much time building the case against Lynn Turner. Prosecutors were planning to charge her with the murders of both Maurice Turner and Roy Thompson.

Lynn Turner went through two different trials; she was first tried in Houston County, Georgia, for the murder of Glenn Turner. A jury found her guilty of her husband's murder on May 14, 2004. A jury in Forsyth County, Georgia, found Turner guilty of Roy Thompson's murder on March 24, 2007. She was sentenced to life imprisonment without possibility of parole.

A Mysterious Death

Lynn Turner died of mysterious circumstances at the Metro State Prison in Atlanta on August 30, 2010. The cause of her death has never been revealed, but there has been strong speculation that she committed suicide behind bars, possibly with poison. Her death was suspicious because she was just 42 years old at the time. Another possibility is that another inmate gave Turner a dose of her own medicine.

THE NURSES WHO KILLED: AUSTRIA'S ANGELS OF DEATH

The scariest of females (or males for that matter) are medical professionals such as nurses or doctors that turn to killing. Such "angels of death" have easy to administer tools of murder in the form of drugs and poisons. Worse, they have access to large numbers of helpless victims and the ability to fool their victims by telling them that the poison is really medicine.

Most killer nurses are lone wolves that operate alone, yet one group of killer nurses operated in a sort of pack: Austria's Lainz Angels of Death. There are many frightening facts about these scary ladies.

They operated in one of the oldest and most modern hospitals in Austria in the heart of the capital of Vienna. They also worked in the center of one of the world's most respected medical systems.

Worst of all, the four women involved may have killed as many as 200 patients over a seven-year period. Like most homicidal nurses, the Angels convinced themselves they were administering euthanasia or mercy killing. Yet accounts of their activities indicate that they degenerated into thrill killers who administered poison for pleasure.

From Angels of Mercy to Sadistic Killers

The angels of death were Maria Gruber, Irene Leidolf, Stephania Meyer, and Waltraud Wagner. All four nurses worked in Pavilion Five of Lainz Hospital, which was filled with elderly patients, many of whom were chronically ill. Three of them—Wagner, Gruber, and Leidolf—were young and just beginning their careers. The fourth, Meyer, was 43 and a grandmother when she joined the pack. Meyer was supposed to be the nurses' house mother.

Much about the angels and their killing spree is unknown, such as exactly when it started. Reportedly, Wagner was the first to kill a patient in 1983 when she killed a man with a fatal dose of morphine. Wagner found she enjoyed killing and soon recruited three colleagues to join her—what she called a "death pavilion."

Wagner was definitely the leader organizing the killing and showing the others how to do it. Worst of all, Wagner began experimenting with ways to make the death more painful. The death pavilion had graduated from mercy killing to plain old-fashioned sadism.

The Water Cure

The worst part of the angels killing spree was that they went out of their way to make their victims' deaths more painful. An example of this was the so-called water cure (named for a vicious torture sometimes inflicted by U.S. soldiers). In the water cure, the nurses would pour water down a victim's nose in order to drown him or her. The result created a painful death that was hard to detect because many elderly people have lungs filled with liquid.

The reasons for the killings were varied; some victims were elderly persons who were in pain and asked for death. Others had simply annoyed the nurses by being annoying or needy patients. Some of the victims may have been put to death for simply soiling or wetting their bed sheets.

Loose Lips Send Angels of Death to Prison

Even though rumors that a serial killer was at work at the Lainz Hospital were swirling around Vienna by 1987, nobody took any action. The nurses were caught by a female stereotype; a penchant for small talk.

In 1989 the death pavilion went out for drinks and had a little too much. The four nurses began chatting about their activities. They even laughed at the discomfort they caused some of their victims.

A doctor enjoying a drink at a nearby table overheard the chilling conversation and became horrified. The frightened physician went straight to the police and told them what he had heard. Unlike the Austrian medical authorities, the Austrian police launched an investigation and discovered that Pavilion Five at Lainz Hospital was literally a house of death rather than a place of healing.

A Nation Shaken to Its Core

Detectives arrested all four members of the death pavilion on April 7, 1989. Wagner soon confessed to 49 murders and made the bizarre statement that she had given 39 patients a free bed with the lord. In jail awaiting trial, Wagner changed her story and claimed that she had only killed ten people. One of her accomplices claimed the body count was actually around 200.

Eventually a jury convicted Wagner of 15 murders and 17 attempted murders and sentenced her to life in prison. Leidolf was also sentenced to prison on five counts of murder. Gruber and Meyer

were sentenced to 15 years in prison for manslaughter and attempted murder.

The case shook the nation of Austria to its core
because of the parallels to one of the horrors of
Nazi Germany. Nazism continues to haunt Austria,
which is known as a highly civilized nation. Hitler
was an Austrian, and the Austrian people cheered
at the Nazi occupation in 1938; unlike other Euro-
pean peoples, they welcomed Hitler's rule.

Parallels to Nazi Euthanasia

The prosecutor at the Angels' trial noted that
their activities mirrored a little known Nazi atrocity
called Aktion T 4. In Aktion T 4, hospital patients
who were considered a drain on German national
resources were put to death. Victims included disabled children, schizophrenics, epileptics, some elderly people, the mentally retarded, and persons
suffering from syphilis. Many of those targeted
were considered un-German; that is, they were obviously not white or not German or Austrian citizens.

Ironically, Hitler himself eventually suspended
or pretended to suspend the program because of
political opposition from the Catholic Church. A
Catholic bishop, Clemens von Galen, openly con-
demned the program as murder in a sermon. It was
1941 and Der Fuhrer needed Catholic soldiers and
officers to fight his war. Unfortunately, Bishop von
Galen didn't extend his criticism to the murder of

Jews, Russians, resistance fighters, and others. When it shut down, Aktion T 4 had claimed 100,000 lives; historians consider the program, which used gas chambers to kill the infirm, a dress rehearsal for the Holocaust of the Jews.

The Death Pavilion Walks Free

It's easy to see why the angels of death so horrified Austrians. Their case continues to generate controversy in the Austrian Republic over 20 years later. In 2008 Austrians were disgusted to learn that authorities were planning to release Waltraud Wagner and Irene Leidolf, who were only in their late 40s. Worse, some reports indicated that the angels would get false identities so they could live a normal life.

In an ironic twist, the efforts to give Austria a humane justice system and distance itself from the Nazis benefited four modern monsters. After World War II Austria had ended the death penalty and made parole available to all prisoners as humanitarian acts. Their release ignited widespread controversy and charges that Austria's justice system was too humane. It's easy to see why: all four members of the death pavilion are now free and living as normal Austrian citizens enjoying the benefits of a compassion they denied their victims.

MARGARET HIGGINS AND CATHERINE FLANNAGAN: THE ORIGINAL BLACK WIDOWS

Some scary women are so infamous that they even add a word or term to the language. Such was the case with the original Black Widows, Margaret Higgins and Catherine Flannagan of Liverpool.

The two women figured out how to use flypaper to dispose of their husbands in order to get their hands on insurance money. The time was the 19th century, and murder for insurance payments was common because it was hard to detect. Corrupt individuals regularly poisoned friends, loved ones, and even complete strangers to get their hands on small insurance settlements.

Sisters Flannagan and Higgins were pretty typical of the serial killers of their day. They used simple chemistry to kill at least five innocent people. Yet the black widows became infamous enough to join other serial killers at Madam Tussaud's famed wax museum in London.

Poisoning Beats Working for a Living

In 1880 Flannagan and Higgins were simply two Irish immigrant sisters living in the dingy British port city of Liverpool. Like many Irish immigrants, the sisters were poor, so they concocted a sick plan to get themselves out of poverty.

The sisters decided to take advantage of so-called burial clubs, a cheap kind of insurance sold to poor people for a few pennies a week. The insurance didn't pay much, but it ensured that even the poorest laborer or cleaning woman could get a decent Christian burial. Margaret and Catherine saw the burial payments as ready cash.

Disturbingly, their first victim was Catherine's own son, John. The women poisoned their own son and nephew for an insurance payment that came to £71 ($107.78). The next victim was Mary Higgins, Margaret's eight-year-old stepdaughter. The black widows were willing to kill innocent children for only a few dollars.

Everybody in the House Was a Target

Like many poor people in 19th century Liverpool, the sisters took in boarders to make a few extra quid. The problem was that they had other ways of making money off the borders: enrolling them in burial clubs, then poisoning them.

The scam was a simple yet horrendous one. The sisters would poison their victims, then give them the cheapest burial possible and pocket the difference. Anybody who set foot in the sisters' house was viewed as a possible payday.

Other victims included Patrick Jennings, another boarder, and his teenage daughter, Margaret. Patrick survived, but Margaret Jennings did not. After Margaret's death the sisters moved to another part of town. They began having money problems, so Margaret Higgins' new husband, Thomas Higgins, conveniently got ill and died. At the time, he had five insurance policies on him.

Incredibly, the local doctor examined Thomas's body and found he had died of dysentery from drinking bad whiskey. Whether the doctor's opinion was honest or based on a bribe is unknown.

Flypaper Is Poison

The black widows were cheap even in their poisoning. To get arsenic, they simply boiled flypaper on the stove. In the 1880s flypaper's main ingredient was arsenic, which was easy to extract.

This time the two had made a serious mistake; Thomas's brother, Patrick, got suspicious about his brother's death. Patrick investigated and discovered the five insurance policies. He immediately went to the police with his suspicions. Constables arrived at the sisters' residence to find Thomas's body in a hearse, ready for transport to the cemetery.

Instead of going to the cemetery, the body was taken to the morgue and examined. Sure enough, investigators found traces of arsenic, and Margaret Higgins was arrested. A constable found a bottle of a mysterious white substance later revealed to be arsenic in Higgins' pocket.

Poisoner on the Run

With Margaret in jail, Catherine tried to make a run for it as police had her other victims. Sure enough, poison was found in their bodies as well. Catherine moved from rooming house to rooming house looking for sanctuary. Eventually a fellow boarder recognized her at dinner and alerted the police. Catherine was arrested and joined her sister in jail.

Testimony at the trial revealed that Catherine, or Catty, Flannagan was the mastermind behind the scheme. Chillingly, Catty Flannagan tried to rat out her sister by offering to testify against her to avoid hanging. Prosecutors resisted the cold blooded offer and managed to secure a conviction without Catty's help.

The sisters were hanged together on March 3, 1884. Their fame would live on in the term Black Widow, revived by the press every time a woman killed her husband. Their crimes may have inspired the activity of at least one other Liverpool killer, the Flypaper Poisoner, Florence Maybrick, who killed her husband ten years later. Like the black widows, Maybrick boiled down flypaper to get arsenic for the crime.

VERA RENCZI: ROMANIA'S BLACK WIDOW AND FEMME FATLE

The public and the media have long been fascinated with the idea of Black Widows, women who kill their lovers or husbands. The scariest Black Widow of all was Romania's Vera Renczi. She killed two husbands, numerous lovers, and her son in a killing spree that made her Romania's No. 1 serial killer.

What's really frightening about Vera Renczi is the number of people that she killed. Some counts suggest that she murdered 25 people, but others indicate that she killed 35. The standard count is 32 lovers and two husbands. Some reports also indicate Renczi killed her son as well.

Spoiled Rich Girl and Insane Jealousy

Despite her murderous ways, Vera Renczi didn't follow the standard pattern of a Black Widow. She didn't kill men for money. She killed out of jealousy and passion. Reports indicate that Renczi, who grew up in Romania and the former Yugoslavia, was a spoiled and self-centered rich girl. She was also very beautiful, but unable to keep a man.

The main motive for Renczi's crimes was jealousy. If a man she was involved with looked at another woman, she would kill him. Her first husband, a much older man, died in a convenient car accident. Renczi remarried, but her second husband vanished and was never seen again.

Renczi soon began having numerous affairs with men that were never seen again. The men would visit her home and simply never come out. Incredibly, she was able to get away with murder at least 32 times before getting caught.

Graveyard in Her Home

Like many promiscuous women, Vera Renczi's downfall was a suspicious wife. Her last lover was a married man. The man's wife decided to follow him to learn who the other woman was.

The wife followed the man to Renczi's house and watched her husband go in, but not come out. After the husband didn't return, the wife went to the police, who finally decided to search Renczi's house in Bucharest. There, they discovered the work of one of the most bizarre serial killers in history.

In the home's basement, the police discovered 32 zinc-lined coffins. Thirty-one of them contained one of Renczi's dead lovers. One contained the body of her missing husband. The results of autopsies indicated that Renczi had killed the men with arsenic that was probably placed in wine.

Jealousy and Insanity

The fact that Vera Renczi was able to get away with so many murders is rather incredible. Even more interesting is the fact that she had coffins delivered to her home. Strangely enough, nobody noticed this bizarre behavior and only one person paid attention to the fact that men entered her home and never came out.

The motive for the murders may have been jealousy or simple boredom. Vera Renczi may have viewed men as toys and simply dispossessed of them when they were no longer interesting. She may have been the ultimate spoiled rich playgirl. An interesting question is the murder of Renczi's son, Lorenzo. Why was he killed? The most likely reason is that he got in the way of his mother's philandering, so he had to go.

It is also interesting to note that Renczi quickly confessed as soon as the police discovered her house of horrors. She put up no defense, offered no excuses, and did not try to blame anybody else for her crimes.

Death in Prison

Vera Renczi's ultimate fate is rather obscure. After being arrested in 1925, she was convicted of 35 murders and sentenced to life in prison. Renczi apparently died in prison at some unknown point. Whether she lived to see World War II and Romania's transition into a brutal Communist dictatorship is unknown. One strong possibility is that the Communists killed Renczi after seizing power in 1945.

Not the Basis for Arsenic and Old Lace

Some people mistakenly assume that Vera Renczi inspired the classic stage play and movie Arsenic and Old Lace, in which two old ladies kill elderly men with poisoned wine and bury their bodies in the basement. That isn't true – the play was actually inspired by Amy Archer-Gilligan, an American killer who poisoned several old men in a nursing home she ran in Newington, Conn. during World War I.

Like Renczi, Archer-Gilligan killed with arsenic and other poisons, yet Archer-Gilligan didn't bury bodies in the basement. Instead, she reported the deaths in hopes of inheriting her victim's money.

Archer-Gilligan was caught when one of his victim's sisters took her story to The Hartford Courant newspaper. The Courant ran a sensational story about Archer-Gilligan's murder factory, which prompted authorities to take action. Archer-Gilligan was arrested, tried, convicted, and sentenced to life imprisonment.

She died in the Connecticut Hospital for the Insane in 1962. Interestingly enough, Archer-Gilligan lived long enough to see her story become a hit play on Broadway and a classic movie starring Cary Grant. Whether the Renczi story, which was publicized in the U.S. press, had any impact on Arsenic and Old Lace's playwright John Kesserling is unknown.

SYLVIA SEEGRIST: TERROR AT THE MALL

The scenario is all too familiar: a troubled loner with a fascination with guns decides to shoot down innocent victims at a public place. But the difference between Sylvia Seegrist and most of these shooters was that she was a woman.

Another difference was that there were plenty of warning signs that Sylvia Seegrist had been planning her deadly rampage at the Springfield Mall near Philadelphia. She had been planning the crime for months and making little secret of it. Many people knew that Sylvia was mentally ill and obsessed with shooting, yet nothing was done until three people lay dead at the mall.

The Crazy Lady at the Mall

Sylvia Seegrist had been grappling with mental illness for at least 10 years before the mall tragedy. She had been diagnosed with schizophrenia when she was 15 and spent time in 12 different mental hospitals. Seegrist was apparently on psychiatric medication at the time of her shooting spree.

Sylvia's mother was so concerned about her daughter's psychotic behavior that she had tried to get her committed. Doctors told Ruth Seegrist that the only way she could get her daughter committed was after a violent incident, yet there had been such an incident in 1984, a year before the shooting spree. Sylvia had tried to choke her own mother to death outside of the Division of Motor Vehicles. Sylvia had been hospitalized for three weeks, then turned loose, even though the doctors admitted she was mentally ill.

There were other signs of violent behavior. Sylvia had to live alone because she attacked anybody who was around her. Worse, she visited the McDonald's franchise in San Ysidro, Calif., the place where James Huberty had gunned down 21 people in July, 1984. Sylvia was apparently inspired by the example set by Huberty.

The young woman was also well known to the people at the mall. Sylvia regularly wandered around the center making strange statements and annoying shoppers. Among other things, she told shoppers that their clothing was too bright.

A Bad Day at the Mall

Sylvia Seegrist's reign of terror began on Oct. 30, 1985, the day before Halloween, when she walked up to the mall wearing fatigues and shiny black boots. Sylvia was also carrying a semiautomatic rifle, but nobody seemed to notice her until she opened fire.

The first target was Edward Seitz, who had the misfortune of being in the mall parking lot when Sylvia drove up in her white Datsun. Sylvia fired two rounds at Edward, but missed him because of the distance. Seitz got away, but the shoppers inside were not so lucky.

Seegrist ran inside and started shooting at anybody she could see. At first, shoppers didn't know what to think – it was 1985 and shooting rampages were rare. It didn't take them long to realize that the woman in the fatigues meant business.

Disturbingly, Sylvia's first targets were children. The first child hit was two-year-old Recife Cosmen, who was standing with his parents outside the Magic Pan restaurant. Recife died instantly, but two other children who were hit managed to survive. Sylvia kept firing and managed to hit four other people, and two of them, Earl Trout and Augustus Ferrara, were killed.

Hero Didn't Realize she was Firing Real Bullets

Sylvia Seegrist's rampage was ended because a man named John Laufer didn't realize she was firing real bullets. Laufer thought the shooting spree was some sort of prank, possibly because it was the day before Halloween. Laufer, a graduate student, simply walked up to Sylvia, grabbed her, and took the gun from her. He then made her walk into a store and sit down while he went looking for the police.

After the incident, Laufer admitted that he didn't know the bullets were not fakes. Had he known they were real, Laufer might not have intervened and many more people might have died. Laufer came back with a security guard, who handcuffed Seegrist. The shooter remained calm until police arrived and took her to jail.

Seegrist's rampage wasn't the worst in U.S. history, but it attracted a lot of attention. It was the first perpetuated by a woman, and it also raised a lot of questions about mental illness and its treatment. People were outraged that such a dangerous individual had been released and allowed to buy a gun and ammunition.

The Debate Still Rages

Despite her history, Sylvia Seegrist was found competent to stand trial. She was eventually found guilty and given three life sentences for murder (one for each dead victim) and seven 10-year sentences for wounding the innocent bystanders. Sylvia is still in state prison in Pennsylvania and will remain there for the rest of her life.

Nearly 30 years after Sylvia's bad day at the mall, the debate about mental illness and guns still rages. Americans are still debating if limiting gun rights and the rights of the mentally ill will prevent such tragedies or not.

ANDREA YATES: KILLER MOTHER

The scariest women of all are mothers that kill their own children. They not only murder; they violate and pervert the most sacred bond of all—motherhood. One of the most frightening killer mothers of all time was Andrea Yates. She drowned five of her own children, including a helpless infant.

Yates' case so startled the American people that it inspired the media and even pop culture. Internet legends even claim that the popular American TV soap opera Desperate Housewives was inspired by Andrea Yates and her horrendous actions. Yates' case shook American society to the core because it touched on such controversial issues as mental illness, religion, and the nature of family.

From Fertile Myrtle to Depression

There were two sides to Andrea Yates, who was born and raised in Houston, Texas. She was a successful young woman, the daughter of immigrants, who was the valedictorian of her high school class, a member of the National Honor Society, and captain of the swim team.

Yet Yates was also a very shy woman who didn't date until she was 23 and met a young man named Rusty Yates. The young couple was serious and intensely religious—they spent much of their time in Bible study and prayer. After marriage, Yates left her job as a nurse and concentrated on having as many children as possible (in compliance with the biblical command to be fruitful and multiply).

Yates was also very reclusive; she had few friends and insisted on home schooling her children. The couple was also heavily influenced by a traveling fundamentalist preacher named Michael Woroiecki, who preached that mothers that had bad children would go to hell. Some observers think these teachings convinced the unstable Yates that she needed to prevent her children from growing up and becoming bad.

Andrea had five children: Noah, John, Paul, Luke, and Mary. She gave them biblical names, but her life wasn't working out. The family had money problems, and Andrea became depressed. She ended up in a mental hospital in 1999 and was prescribed the antidepressant Haldol. Her husband eventually talked her out of taking Haldol for religious reasons.

A Weird Family Life and Murder

The Yates' family life was certainly weird. They lived in an old school bus for a number of years, then in 2000 they returned to a more normal suburban life in Houston and bought a home.

The new life didn't work out and became a true nightmare on June 20, 2001. On that day Rusty left for his job at NASA as he normally did. After he left the home, Andrea turned a normal activity, bathing her five children, into a ritual of death.

While her children were eating their cereal, Andrea went into the bathroom and filled the tub with water. She then lured each of them into the bathroom and held them face down in the water until they were dead. Andrea covered each of the bodies with a sheet after drowning them. One of them, six-month-old Mary, she took out of her bassinet and drowned. The last to go was five-year-old Noah, whose body she left floating in the tub.

After the killings, Andrea called the police and told the operator that she had killed her children. When officers came to her home, they discovered a true scene of horror that included Noah's body floating in a filthy tub with water full of urine, vomit, and feces. Andrea was arrested and taken to police headquarters. Rusty came home from work and was unable to get into his own home because it was now a crime scene.

Circus in the Court Room and Weird Testimony

Andrea Yates was tried twice for her horrible crimes in two different trials that deteriorated into media circuses. The first trial, held in 2002, hinged on the issue of Andrea Yates' sanity.

Yates' attorneys tried to prove that she was insane, which would protect her from the death penalty. Prosecutors tried to prove that Yates was sane, which would make her eligible for the death penalty. The prosecution prevailed in the first trial with the help of a prominent witness, a psychiatrist named Park Dietz. Dietz, a professional witness who had helped prosecutors prove that cannibal serial killer Jeffrey Dahmer and the Unabomber were sane, did the same for Andrea.

There was only one problem—part of Dietz's testimony was false. Dietz claimed that Yates was inspired by an episode of the popular TV police procedural Law & Order in which a woman drowned her children in a bathtub. There was no such episode; Dietz's testimony was poorly researched and flawed, and a court threw it out and overturned Yates' convictions on five counts of first-degree murder in January 2005.

Saved from the Death Penalty

The overturning of the first conviction saved Andrea Yates from the death penalty but not from herself. In July 2006 a second jury, which hadn't heard from Dietz, found Andrea Yates not guilty by reason of insanity and sentenced her to life in prison.

Yates is currently being held in the Kerrville State Hospital in Texas. She participates in the Yates Children Memorial Fund, which tries to help families deal with mental illness and spread the word about postpartum depression, which she blames for her homicidal behavior. Rusty Yates still lives in the family home in Houston. Andrea Yates will stay in Texas state prisons for a long time to come without a pardon. She won't be eligible for parole until the year 2041, when she will be 77 years old.

CORDELIA BOTKIN: THE TRANSCONTINENTAL POISONER

What makes Cordelia Botkin so scary is that she managed to murder two people who were clear across the United States from her. Botkin lived in San Francisco at the time of the murders, but her victims lived in Dover, Delaware, on the East Coast.

Botkin's case was a colorful one because she was having an affair with a popular and dashing newspaper correspondent named John P. Dunning at the time of the murders. Unlike most turn of the 20th century poisoners, Botkin killed for love rather than money. Poisoning was a common form of murder for women killers in the late 19th century, but they usually murdered for the insurance money or inheritance.

Botkin's motive was more romantic; in an age before divorce, she wanted to be free to be with and marry her lover. Murder was apparently the only way that she could achieve this end and prevent her younger lover from going back to his more socially prominent wife.

The Married Woman and the Correspondent

There wasn't that much that was attractive or unusual about Cordelia Botkin; she was an overweight housewife from Stockton, California. Botkin had been born in Missouri and grew up in California. At some point in the 1870s or 1880s she had married a man with the unusual name of Welcome Botkin and had one son.

Cordelia's routine life changed completely in 1895 when she met an exciting younger man named John P. Dunning while bicycling in San Francisco's Golden Gate Park. Dunning was only 31 and he had a very glamorous job; he was a foreign correspondent for the Associated Press. In the late 19th Century and the first half of the 20th Century newspaper reporters and correspondents were often viewed as larger than life heroes who led lives of adventure.

Dunning was famous because he had covered a typhoon in Samoa as well as the Spanish American War. There was only one problem with Dunning; he was already married to another woman—Mary Elizabeth Pennington Dunning. She was the daughter of a congressman, but she was also on the other side of the country in Dover, Delaware.

Death through the Mail

By 1898 Cordelia Botkin had left her husband and moved in with Dunning at the Victoria Hotel in San Francisco. The situation wasn't ideal because there was no divorce and women who lived with men that weren't their husband were viewed as whores at the time. There was always the possibility that Dunning would go back to his wealthier wife at any time.

That eventually happened in 1898 when Dunning, who was out of work and unable to pay his gambling debts, returned to the Associated Press and his wife. He told Cordelia that he would return to his wife in Dover after covering the Spanish American War in Cuba rather than San Francisco.

Cordelia tried to correct this situation first by sending Mary Elizabeth threatening notes. At some point Botkin had discovered that Mary Elizabeth had a sweet tooth; she decided to take advantage of this weakness.

On August 9, 1899, Mary Elizabeth Dunning received a special gift through the mail: a box of candy. Mrs. Dunning gave some of the candy to her older sister Harriet Deane then tried some herself. Both sisters died from arsenic poisoning shortly after. Four other people who tried the candy got sick. Botkin sent a grotesque note with the poisoned candy. It said: "With love to yourself and baby," and "passionately fond of candy."

Long Distance Arrest and Trial

The mysterious deaths of his healthy daughters made John Pennington, Dunning's father-in-law, suspicious. Pennington searched the home and found the candy and some threatening letters from Botkin. Pennington then contacted a state chemist, who analyzed the candy and discovered it contained deadly amounts of arsenic.

Arsenic is a particularly cruel poison because it can cause victims to literally vomit themselves to death. This fact can work to a poisoners' benefit because victims often purge the poison from their bodies before they die. Unfortunately, high amounts of arsenic can destroy large numbers of cells that can lead to death.

The poisoned candy led to a coroner's inquest; the inquest determined that the two women had been murdered. The Dover police investigated and discovered that the candy had been mailed from San Francisco; Mrs. Botkin was apparently stupid enough to leave a postmark on the package she had mailed. Two Dover cops took the poisoned candy and other evidence to San Francisco.

After examining the evidence, veteran detective and San Francisco police chief I. W. Lees tracked down the shop that sold the candy. Shop employees gave Lees Botkin's name, and he tracked her down at her sister's house and arrested her. Even though the deaths had occurred in Delaware, Botkin was tried in California; the first conviction was dismissed, but she was successfully retried in 1904.

She Murdered for a Thief and a Failure

Cordelia Botkin was sentenced to life in prison and died at San Quentin in 1910. Interestingly enough, she survived John Dunning by two years; he died in 1908 in Philadelphia. By then he was a drunken wreck who couldn't find work. Dunning couldn't find work because it became known that he had embezzled $4,000 from the Associated Press to pay his gambling debts. Nobody would hire the once famous correspondent after that bit of information came out.

The most ironic aspect of Cordelia Botkin's crimes was that she committed them for the love of man who was unfaithful, a gambling addict, a failure in his career and a thief. The cause of Dunning's death isn't known; there's a good chance he committed suicide because his journalism career was in ruins.

DOROTHEA PUENTE: THE BOARDING HOUSE OF DEATH

Dorothea Puente's story is so strange and sensational that it sounds like a movie plot. A friendly little old lady living in a nice house in a quiet neighborhood takes in boarders that turn up dead in the yard or the basement. In fact, it is the plot of the classic American movie and stage play, Arsenic and Old Lace, in which a man discovers that his kindly elderly aunts are murdering tenants and burying their bodies in the basement.

Arsenic and Old Lace is a comedy, but Dorothea Puente's case was more like a horror movie. In fact, it was far more frightening than most horror movies. Unlike movie serial killers, Puente targeted helpless people, such as the elderly and the mentally handicapped, for death. Worse, her motive was very simple and despicable; she killed the helpless in order to steal their welfare and social security checks.

Tenants would move into Dorothea Puente's boarding house in Sacramento, but they would never move out. Yet their checks would still arrive in the mail and find their way into Dorothea's bank account. What's worse was that Dorothea used the welfare money intended to help the poor to pay for such luxuries as face-lifts and $110 bottles of perfume.

A Lifelong Criminal

Residents of F Street in Sacramento knew Dorothea Puente as a kindly old woman who ran a rooming house and fed stray cats. What they didn't realize was that Dorothea was a professional criminal with a lifelong history of fraud and possibly murder.

Dorothea grew up poor during the Depression in Redlands, California. Her parents, who were migrant farm workers, both died when she was a girl, so she ended up in an orphanage. She ran away at 16 and married a GI returning from World War II, then had two children. By the late 1940s Dorothea had turned to check fraud and landed in jail.

By 1960 Dorothea was arrested in Sacramento for running a brothel. After serving jail time for prostitution, Dorothea turned to a more loathsome racket; preying on the elderly and disabled. She became a nurse's aide and a boarding home operator not to help the elderly and disabled but because they were easier to steal from.

The Boarding House of Death Opens

By 1981 Dorothea Puente had been living in a 16-room Victorian mansion at 2100 F Street in Sacramento for years. She supported herself by forging benefit checks stolen from older men she met in bars. When an arrest ended that racket, Puente began taking in boarders.

One of Puente's first boarders was her business partner, Ruth Munroe, who moved into the house in the spring of 1982. Munroe soon died of a drug overdose and left Puente an inheritance that included $6,000 in cash. The coroner ruled the death a suicide even though Puente had just been arrested for drugging an elderly man and looting his home.

Puente went to state prison for three years after police discovered that activity. At the time of her arrest, a judge ordered Puente to stay away from the elderly and government checks issued to others. She obviously ignored the judge's recommendations.

The Best Care the System Can Offer

Puente resumed her killing spree almost as soon as she got out of prison. She had been writing to a 77-year-old man named Everson Gillmouth. Gillmouth told his sister that he was going to Sacramento to marry Puente. Instead of marriage, Puente murdered Gillmouth and dumped his body next to the Sacramento River in a homemade coffin. Gillmouth was killed as soon as he had made Puente a signatory on his checking account. That enabled her to steal his pension payments. Gillmouth's body would not be identified until three years later, when Puente was caught.

Despite her criminal record, Puente was able to start talking social workers into placing elderly, disabled, and drug-addicted patients into her home as tenants. A social worker said Puente provided the best care the system could offer. In reality, Puente was murdering the tenants and burying them in her backyard.

What's worse is that the stench from the rotting corpses was so bad that the neighbors had to close their windows. Puente tried to cover up the smell with lime, but it got worse. Yet nobody realized that anything was wrong, even though there were now seven corpses buried in her yard.

Caught by Accident

Puente was finally caught when police detective John Cabrera paid her a visit. Cabrera was looking for Burt Montoya, a developmentally disabled schizophrenic, who had been reported missing by his social worker. Cabrera and his colleagues didn't notice anything unusual inside, but they saw that the garden had been dug up.

Guided more by his instincts than anything else, Cabrera started digging in the garden. He soon uncovered a human corpse. The house was now a crime scene, and the next day a team of forensic anthropologists was digging up the garden. They eventually found seven corpses in the yard of the house, which was just two blocks from the California governor's mansion.

Incredibly, police left Puente free to watch the scene and then go to a nearby hotel for coffee. Instead of going to the hotel, Puente fled to Los Angeles, where she was arrested at a fleabag hotel near that city's skid row. She was already reportedly targeting men in bars for theft when she was arrested in LA. A man Dorothea met in a bar tipped police off to her location after seeing her face on TV.

Cooking with a Serial Killer

Dorothea Puente was sentenced to life in prison without possibility of parole. She stayed in California prisons until her death from natural causes in 2011 when she was 82. The murderous caregiver received better care in prison than she had provided for the elderly.

Puente also became an author while she was in prison; in 2004 her pen pal, Shane Bugbee, published a book he called Cooking with a Serial Killer. The book contained 50 recipes that Puente had sent to Bugbee from her prison cell. It isn't clear if the book contained Puente's recipes for poison or not.

GRISELDA BLANCO: THE GODMOTHER OF COCAINE AND BLACK WIDOW

In the world of organized crime and drug dealing, Colombia's Griselda Blanco was definitely a pioneer. The grandmother is credited with being one of the founders of the Medellin cartel, a pioneer in smuggling cocaine from Columbia to the U.S., a major player in Miami's drug wars, and one of the 10 richest drug dealers in history.

Unlike most female criminals, Griselda Blanco was a major league gangster who ordered rivals rubbed out, ran rackets, and built up a huge fortune. She also delighted in the nickname "Godmother" and even named her son Michael

Corleone after the character from the Godfather movies.

Blanco's life has much in common with famous male gangsters like Bugsy Siegel; she spent time in federal prison, got targeted by U.S. authorities, and was eventually gunned down on a public street. In fact, Blanco became so famous that a Hollywood movie based on her life is in preproduction. Online rumors indicate that Jennifer Lopez is among the stars chasing the role. Mark Wahlberg is supposed to be producing the picture.

A Pioneer in the Cocaine Industry

Like many male gangsters, Griselda Blanco grew up poor in a violent place and time: Colombia during the 1960s and '70s. A vicious civil war was raging between Communist guerrillas and right-wing death squads in the country. The conflict, known locally as La Violencia, was compounded by a growing drug trade with the United States and Western Europe.

In common with legendary male gangsters, Griselda started her career early. A legend in her hometown of Medellin claims that she kidnapped a young boy for ransom when she was 11. When the boy's parents wouldn't pay, she reportedly killed him.

Griselda found her true life calling when she started hanging around with a street punk and car thief named Pablo Escobar. At the time she was a petty criminal who was engaged in counterfeiting and prostitution. She also married a number of times and earned the nickname "Black Widow" for murdering husbands.

Like Escobar, Griselda was attracted by the big money in the cocaine trade. It was the 1970s, and the white powder could quickly be turned into wealth, provided you could get it to the U.S. or Europe. Griselda solved this problem by opening a women's underwear factory, and the underwear contained secret compartments so female mules could use it to move cocaine to the U.S.

At this time, some experts credit her with inventing a popular assassination technique by having a killer ride on a motorcycle and blast enemies with a machine gun. She had a terrible temper and was believed to have ordered dozens of killings.

Moving to America

Like many ambitious Latin Americans, Griselda Blanco decided to immigrate to the United States. She moved to Queens, N.Y. (which, not coincidently, is the center of Mafia activity in the United States) to direct smuggling operations.

One of her first activities in the United States was to try and smuggle six kilos of cocaine into the U.S. on the sailing ship Gloria. The Colombian government had sent the Gloria to New York to celebrate the Bicentennial of the United States in 1976. Blanco was also among the defendants in the first major cocaine trafficking indictment handed down by federal prosecutors in New York City.

Now a fugitive, Blanco moved to Miami and helped turn the resort city into America's crime capitol. She imported vast amounts of cocaine into the city and ordered dozens of killings. The most colorful was the stabbing of a rival cocaine smuggler with a bayonet at Miami International Airport. The Cocaine Wars added a new character to American popular culture, the trigger-happy Colombian cocaine cowboy.

Fighting Uncle Sam

Griselda Blanco could eliminate rival drug lords, but she was no match for Uncle Sam. Like Al Capone, she became a target of the U.S. Justice Department, and as in the case of Big Al, Uncle Sam assembled a special team of elite untouchable agents dedicated to bringing her down.

The elite team CENTAC 26 caught Griselda by arresting her top hit man, Jorge Rivi Ayala. He ratted Blanco out and enabled prosecutors to file three murder charges against her. CENTAC 26 agents tracked her down and arrested her in California. The murder charges were eventually dropped because a phone sex scandal involving Ayala and secretaries embarrassed the federal prosecutor.

Instead, Blanco pleaded guilty to three second-degree murder charges. She was sentenced to 20 years in federal prison. In prison, Blanco was the center of a bizarre rumor that she was planning to have John F. Kennedy Jr. kidnapped. She hoped to use the life of the heir to Camelot as a bargaining chip to win her release. The plot never materialized and ended up as fodder for tabloid reporters.

Paying a High Price for Fame and Fortune

Griselda Blanco, like most famous gangsters, paid a high price for fame and fortune. She ended up serving 16 years in a federal prison. Two of her four sons were murdered in Colombia while she was in prison. In 2004, Blanco was released from federal prison and deported to Colombia.

There, she tried to live a quiet life paid for by her ill-gotten gains. Blanco lived in an expensive neighborhood and claimed that she was no longer involved in organized crime. In early September 2012, Blanco went to a butcher shop in Medellin and bought $165 worth of meat. When she walked out of the shop, the former godmother was gunned down by a man on a motorcycle with a ma-chine pistol. In an ironic development worthy of a gangster movie, Blanco was killed with an assassi-nation technique she had reputedly pioneered.

Griselda Blanco may be dead, but the family business goes on. Her son, Michael Corleone Blan-co, was recently arrested on charges of cocaine smuggling.

JANE TOPPAN: PIONEER KILLER NURSE

The scariest female killers of all are the killer nurses. These ladies are supposed to be angels of mercy, but they are really angels of death. Such murderesses are particularly frightening because they target helpless victims, and they often administer deadly poison as medicine. Their victims rarely realize they are targeted for death.

To add to the nightmare, most killer nurses claim to be helping their victims or putting them out of their misery. In reality though, most such killers enjoy the perverse power that control over life and death brings them.

The first and one of the scariest killer nurses was a woman from Massachusetts named Jane

Toppan. Toppan achieved nationwide fame in the early 1900s by killing dozens of innocent people with various cocktails of drugs. Like many poisoners, Toppan experimented on her victims in an attempt to concoct the perfect poison.

From Orphan Girl to Killer Nurse

Like many infamous criminals, Jane Toppan tried to conceal her true identity and background. Her real name was Honora Kelly, and her parents were poor Irish Catholics. Honora's mother died young, and her father, an alcoholic, was unable to support the family; he eventually dumped his two daughters at an orphanage and disappeared.

Honora Kelly took the more American name Jane Toppan while working for a middle class family as a servant girl. At the time (the 1860s) the Irish were looked down upon as poor and ignorant. After shedding her roots, Toppan started climbing the social ladder by studying to be a nurse at Cambridge Hospital.

What's most frightening about Jane Toppan is that she did not study nursing to help people or heal the sick. In later years, Toppan admitted freely that her real purpose in studying nursing was to learn how to kill people. Toppan began experimenting on patients by giving them large doses of drugs to see what would happen. Strangely enough, she would often hold the patients close while they died.

Murder Spree and Celebrity

The authorities at Cambridge Hospital became suspicious of Toppan, but they didn't report her to the authorities. They simply fired her, so she went on to the Massachusetts General Hospital, where she killed several more innocent people. After a while Toppan was banned from hospitals, but she found work as a private nurse.

In 1895 Toppan started killing people outside the hospital as well, poisoning her landlords and her own foster sister, Elizabeth. Like England's Dr. Death, Harold Shipman, a century later, Toppan began stealing from her patients as well as killing them.

The end came for Toppan in 1901 when she targeted the Davis family of Catumet, Massachusetts, for death. Davis first killed the wife of an elderly man named Alden Davis then moved in with the Davis family. Davis's two daughters soon died and finally Davis himself.

Arrest and Insanity

Jane Toppan's behavior had become particularly bizarre at this time. She tried to seduce her late foster sister's husband by poisoning him and his sister. The ruse didn't work, and her brother-in-law threw her out of the house.

Meanwhile Alden Davis's suspicious relatives talked police into having a toxicology exam done on the body of one of Davis's daughters, Jane Gibbs. The exam proved that Gibbs had been poisoned to death. Police, acting on this tip, began surveillance of Jane Toppan. Her actions were suspicious enough for officers to arrest her on October 26, 1901.

Toppan was put on trial in 1902 and became one of the first serial killers to escape the death penalty through the insanity defense. Jurors found her not guilty by reason of insanity and committed the nurse to the state insane asylum for life.

From Serial Killer to Celebrity

It was at this time that Toppan became the focus of so-called yellow journalism. Reporters for press baron William Randolph Hearst's New York Journal tried to boost circulation by printing what they claimed to be Toppan's "confession." The account published in The Journal claimed that Toppan had confessed to killing 31 people.

Almost immediately doubt was thrown on the account because Hearst, who was locked in a brutal circulation battle with rivals, was not above making up sensational stories to sell newspapers. The account claimed to come from Toppan's lawyer.

A strong possibility is that Hearst's reporters simply paid the lawyer for the account. If that happened, it would be a clear violation of attorney cli-

ent privilege and blatantly illegal. Since nobody
was punished for the confession, it isn't clear where
it came from.

Death in the Asylum

Jane Toppan was one of the few serial killers
who lived to a ripe old age. She died in the Taun-
ton Insane Hospital in Massachusetts in 1938 when
she was 81 years old. The woman who once reportedly boasted that her life's mission was to
"have killed more helpless people than any other
man or woman who ever lived" died quietly of natural causes.

KARLA FAYE TUCKER: PICKAXE KILLER AND BORN AGAIN CHRISTIAN

Few murderers have attracted as much attention as Karla Faye Tucker, the first woman executed in the state of Texas since the Civil War. To her critics, Tucker was a crazed cold-blooded killer who robbed defenseless people and murdered them with a pickaxe. Yet to legions of supporters, Tucker was an admirable person because of her professed conversion to born again Christianity.

Tucker's case became a political lightning rod because many of those opposed to her execution were conservative Christians who normally supported the death penalty. Many of the born again ended up siding with anti-death penalty leftists in an attempt to save her life.

If any case ever came to symbolize the debate over the death penalty, it was Tucker's. The case also raised serious moral questions and accusations of hypocrisy against Tucker's supporters and detractors alike.

A Girl who Grew up Too Fast

If any little girl ever grew up too fast, it was Karla Faye Tucker. Reports indicate that she started smoking marijuana before she was 10 years old. Karla was also having sex with boys as early as junior high school. She was able to do this because there was little discipline in the Tucker family home – her parents were constantly separating and getting back together again.

To make matters worse, Karla's mother, Carolyn, was in a rock group and spent her time following bands on tour. Carolyn apparently paid for her roving lifestyle through prostitution.

By the time she was in her teens, Karla had found a new family to hang out with, the Bandidos, a notorious motorcycle gang. Karla hung around the gang's clubhouse and participated in orgies there. By the time she was 20, Karla was a hardened gang moll who traded sex to the vicious criminals for drugs. Like her mother, Karla also worked as a prostitute.

Motorcycle in the Living Room Leads to Murder

Karla Faye Tucker's troubles really began when she hooked up with a biker and neighborhood drug dealer named Danny Garrett. She hung around Garrett because he gave her free drugs and didn't object to her prostitution.

Karla Faye Tucker and Danny Garrett graduated from petty criminals to vicious murderers on June 13, 1983. The two were invited to a drugs and sex party where they ran into somebody that Karla hated, another biker named Jerry Lynn Dean. Karla was mad at Dean because she once caught him working on his motorcycle in the living room of her Houston apartment.

After the party, Karla and Danny decided to get even with Dean and his wife, Shawn, by stealing the only valuable thing Dean owned, his Harley Davidson motorcycle (or hog, a biker's most prized possession). To work up courage for their plan, the two decided to get high on drugs first. The two recruited another petty crook named Jimmy Leibrant to act as lookout and headed for Dean's residence.

Banshee with a Pickaxe

It isn't clear whether Karla and Danny simply intended to rob Dean or kill him. Circumstances indicate that they planned to kill Dean – they went to his home in the middle of the night with a shotgun and a revolver.

When the two entered Dean's home, they found his disassembled motorcycle and several tools, including a pickaxe and a shovel, in the living room. When Dean surprised them, Garrett picked up a hammer and beat him in the head with it. Garrett's blows were so savage that he nearly knocked Dean's head off.

Karla became disappointed because she wasn't participating in the fun. So she picked up the pickaxe and went into Dean's bedroom in search of another victim. Karla found a woman named Deborah Thornton in the bedroom and began chopping her up with the pickaxe. Thornton was killed simply because she was in the wrong place at the wrong time. It isn't even clear if Karla knew Thornton.

What is clear is that Karla hit Thornton so many times she turned her body to mush. If that wasn't bad enough, Danny stood there cheering on Karla. Once she was done with Thornton, Karla went back into the living room and hit Dean with the pickaxe 20 times. Since he was already unconscious, Dean had no way to defend himself.

Arrest Trial and Repentance

After the killings, Danny and Karla stole Dean's motorcycle parts and fled. The bodies were discovered by a co-worker of Dean's who was looking for a ride. Police arrested the two shortly after the bodies were discovered. They probably tracked them down when they tried to sell the stolen motorcycle parts.

Karla Faye Tucker's trial was uneventful. She pleaded not guilty and was quickly convicted. Tucker's life changed when she started reading the Bible in prison. The Bible readings convinced her to become a Christian and marry Dana Lane Brown, a prison chaplain.

After her conversion, Tucker's case began attracting international attention. Several famous people, including Pope John Paul II, the Prime Minister of Italy, then Speaker of the U.S. House of Representatives Newt Gingrich (a death penalty supporter), and controversial TV preacher Pat Robertson asked Texas Governor George W. Bush for clemency. Even Deborah Thornton's brother, Ronald Carlson, joined the pleas.

Bush was not swayed, and on Feb. 2, 1998, Tucker was flown from Gatesville, Texas to the state's death row in Huntsville. She was executed the next day in front of four witnesses. The witnesses reported that the former biker chick praised Jesus as she met her fate. She was the first woman executed in the Lone Star State since axe murderer Chipita Rodriguez was hanged in 1863.

The controversy surrounding her execution did not die with Karla Faye Tucker. Some observers think George W. Bush's refusal to commute her sentence helped him advance his political career to the White House in 2000.

CARIL ANN FUGATE: HALF OF A DEADLY DUO

Caril Ann Fugate became a legend when she was just 14 years old. She and her boyfriend became the most notorious killer couple to terrorize the United States since Bonnie and Clyde. Their robbery spree sowed chaos across Nebraska and became part of American popular culture.

Fugate was also one of the few notorious murderers who was able to escape and live a quiet life in later years. Her case still evokes controversy in Nebraska, where her name will be forever linked with that of the state's most famous outlaw, Charles Starkweather.

In the 1950s Charles Starkweather and Caril Ann Fugate were as feared as Bonnie and Clyde had been in depression era Texas. In some ways,

Fugate and Starkweather's crimes were more frightening because they went on the rampage in a time of relative peace and prosperity for average Americans. Unlike Bonnie and Clyde, Starkweather and Fugate targeted average people in their homes rather than banks.

A Little Girl from a Small Town

In 1958 Caril Anne Fugate and her family were living a quiet life in Lincoln, Nebraska. The only thing odd about the 14-year-old girl was her relationship with an older loser named Charles Starkweather. Starkweather, a high school dropout, was definitely going nowhere; he was a day laborer who unloaded newspaper trucks for a living.

Starkweather was also something of a punk who liked to emulate movie star James Dean's character in the iconic film Rebel without a Cause. Eventually Starkweather lost his job and ended up working on a garbage truck. He began plotting bank robberies and scheming to get revenge on people he hated.

Charles and Caril's relationship changed when he told her that he had killed and robbed gas station attendant Robert Colvert. After making this confession, the young couple went to Fugate's house. Once there Charles shot and killed Fugate's mother, stepfather, and sister with a rifle. He then reportedly stabbed and strangled Fugate's two-year-old sister, Betty Jean.

Deadly Duo on the Rampage

Caril Ann Fugate may not have taken part in the murder of her family, but she certainly witnessed it. Caril could have probably run away or called for help; instead, she and Charles lived in the Fugate family home for seven days with her family's bodies dumped out in the back yard.

Finally, Fugate's grandmother got suspicious and alerted the police. By then Charles and Caril had driven to Bennet, Nebraska. Once there Starkweather killed 70-year-old farmer August Meyer with a shotgun.

The next crime was even more violent, brutal, and senseless. Starkweather and Fugate hijacked a teenaged couple named Robert Jensen and Carol King. The duo drove their victims to a remote storm cellar. Once there, Starkweather shot Jensen and tried to rape King. Fugate then shot King and mutilated her genitals.

Stabbing Victims in Their Own Home

Strangely enough, Charles Starkweather never put his plans of bank robbery into action. Instead, he and Fugate drove into Lincoln, where they entered the home of the wealthy Ward family. Once there, they stabbed the woman of the house, Clara Ward, and her maid, Lillian Fencl, to death. Then they waited in ambush for Clara's husband, Lauer Ward, to come home; when he came home, Charles shot Ward and stole his car.

Nebraska had finally become too hot for the two. Citizens were in a panic, police were conducting a house-to-house search of Lincoln, and the governor was talking of calling out the National Guard.

The two fled to Douglas, Wyoming, where Charles Starkweather shot traveling salesman Merle Collison and stole his car. Starkweather wasn't able to start Collison's car after it stalled. Instead, the murder led to the arrest of the fugitives.

Partners in Crime Turn on Each Other

The next series of events makes the story of Caril Ann Fugate all the more confusing. A deputy sheriff pulled up to help the young couple; Charles reached for his rifle while Caril ran to the lawman and surrendered. She yelled, "That's Starkweather."

Starkweather managed to get the car going and drove off at 100 miles per hour. He may have been faster than the police, but he wasn't faster than the rifle bullet a deputy fired into his car. Starkweather stopped and was arrested by deputies when he realized that he was bleeding.

After her arrest, Fugate claimed she was Starkweather's hostage. Starkweather claimed that she was his partner in crime and willingly participated in some of the murders. It is still impossible to tell which one of them was telling the truth.

Lasting Fame and Controversy

Caril Anne Fugate and Charles Starkweather were tried separately for their crimes. Starkweather was sentenced to death and died in the electric chair at the Nebraska State Penitentiary in 1959.

Caril Fugate was sentenced to life in prison but was paroled in a controversial decision in 1976. The Daily Beast website reported that she now lives quietly in a small town in Michigan, where she is married to a machinist. Fugate also worked as a janitor in a state hospital in Michigan for 30 years. Fugate has only talked publicly about her life twice.

Caril Fugate has been able to live her life quietly despite a great deal of fame. Her crime spree inspired three movies, including the critically acclaimed Badlands, which helped launch the careers of Sissy Spacek and Martin Sheen in 1973. It also inspired Bruce Springsteen's song, Nebraska. Unlike Bonnie Parker, Caril Fugate was able to outlive both fame and infamy.

BLANCHE TAYLOR MOORE: SERIAL BLACK WIDOW

Black widows, or women who murder their husbands and lovers usually through poison, rarely face the death penalty. That's why the case of North Carolina native Blanche Taylor Moore is so unusual. Moore found herself on death row for poisoning two husbands, a boyfriend, a pastor, and her mother-in-law in a killing spree that lasted more than 20 years.

Like most black widows, Moore was motivated by greed. She poisoned those around her so she could get her hands on their money. Worst of all, she was able to get away with the killings for two decades.

Grocery Store Clerk and Murderer

Like most black widows, Blanche Moore presented two different sides to the world. In public,
she was a sweet Christian lady who worked at the
local Kroger grocery store and sang in the church
choir. In private, she was a cold-blooded killer who
poisoned those who got in her way.

Blanche Moore grew up poor in Alamance
County, N.C. Her father was a salesman and mill
worker, and Blanche herself went to work at Kroger right out of high school and stayed there for 30
years. When she was 19, Blanche married James
Taylor, who had just returned from the Korean
War.

Taylor died in 1968 when he was 40. The death
was declared a heart attack, and Blanche was free
to date a more eligible man, Raymond C. Reid, the
manager of the Kroger store where she worked.
Taylor was just a furniture restorer, while Reid
made a much better income. In 1970, Taylor's
mother, Isla, whom Blanche inherited money from,
died as well.

Killing the Preacher

Blanche maintained her relationship with Raymond C. Reid until 1986. By then, Reid was no
longer of use to her. She had left the job at Kroger
and fallen in love with another man, the Reverend
Dwight Moore. Shortly after she had met Moore,

Reid developed a very bad case of the shingles. He was eventually hospitalized and died.

Blanche was now free to date Reverend Moore, a local minister. Reverend Moore eventually married her, which was a mistake. In 1988 Blanche bought the Reverend a chicken sandwich, and after eating the sandwich Moore became very sick and went to the hospital. Doctors at the hospital diagnosed arsenic poisoning. It was later determined that the Reverend had one of the worst cases of arsenic poisoning ever contracted.

Botched Poisoning Leads to Capture

The doctors who had treated Reverend Moore notified the North Carolina Bureau of Investigation, which began looking into Blanche. When investigators discovered that Blanche's first husband had died, they started looking into her past.

The bodies of Reid, Blanche's father, mother-in-law, and ex-husband were all exhumed and tested for arsenic. Investigators determined that James Taylor, Reid, and Isla Taylor had all died of arsenic poisoning. The investigation turned up some chilling details, including the fact that Blanche fed Reid arsenic-laced pudding while he was in the hospital because of earlier arsenic poisoning.

The investigators also found that a resident at Baptist Hospital in Winston-Salem, N.C. had suspected arsenic poisoning in Reid's case, but failed to pass test results onto his superiors. That means that the poisoning was never reported. Reid's family later sued Baptist Hospital, blaming it for his death.

Trial, Fame and Over Twenty Years on Death Row

Police acting on information gathered by the North Carolina Bureau of Investigation arrested Blanche Taylor Moore on July 18, 1989. She was charged with first-degree murder in the death of Raymond Reid. Prosecutors didn't charge her with attempted murder in Moore's case because they didn't have enough evidence.

During a trial in 1990 the prosecutors proved that Moore had visited Reid in the hospital dozens of times and brought food. She was also in a position to profit from Reid's death as the executor of his estate. The testimony of the cold-blooded behavior convinced the jury to find Moore guilty and the judge to sentence her to death by lethal injection in 1991.

Her trial sparked nationwide interest and fascination. It also inspired a television movie called The Black Widow Murders: The Blanche Taylor Moore Story. In the movie, Moore was played by Elizabeth Montgomery of Bewitched fame, not another major situation comedy star Mary Tyler Moore.

Today, over 23 years later, Blanche Taylor Moore is still on death row – her execution has been delayed by constant legal maneuvering. Recent media reports indicate that Blanche Taylor Moore has received medical treatment to keep her alive at the taxpayers' expense so she might someday be executed.

In another example of the twisted logic that exemplifies the American legal system, Blanche Taylor Moore, who is white, has filed a motion claiming that she is a victim of racism because she was sentenced to death. One thing is certain though, the Reverend Moore survived the arsenic-poisoning attempt – he didn't die until 2013.

JANIE LOU GIBBS: SHE POISONED HER ENTIRE FAMILY

Some of the most terrifying entries in the roll call of scary women go to those ladies who destroy their entire families. On this list, Janie Lou Gibbs is among the most chilling and cold blooded. She poisoned three of her children, her husband, and her grandson to get the insurance money.

This monster valued the fast buck more than her whole family. Then, to make her crimes particularly repugnant and hypocritical, she donated part of the money she made to the church. Obviously, Janie Lou Gibbs had missed the Ten Commandments and the part about "Thou Shall Not Kill" during her Bible readings.

A Southern Family Tragedy

Janie Lou Gibbs grew up poor in the southern backwater of Cordele, Georgia. Her life was a hard one; she married when she was just 15, and she was a grandmother by the time she was 35. Since Janie's husband was unable to make enough money to support the family, Janie augmented the family income by running a daycare center in her home.

Gibbs' life attracted little attention until 1966, when strange deaths started plaguing the Gibbs family. The first to die was Gibbs' husband, Charles, who succumbed in January 1966. The next was her 13-year-old son, Marvin, who was rushed to the hospital in 1966. Doctors diagnosed a kidney disease but were unable to save the boy. Five months later Marvin's older brother, Melvin, who was 16, became sick with liver disease and died as well.

Incredibly, Gibbs was able to block tests and autopsies by insurance investigators that could have showed the true cause of the deaths. Then, with two sons in their graves, the monster turned on her own infant grandson.

Poisoning an Infant

Janie Lou Gibbs' eldest son, Roger, and his wife were living with his parents when their son, Ronnie Edward, was born. Ronnie was a healthy baby at birth, but he too soon came down with the mysterious liver disease and passed away. This time doctors performed an autopsy but couldn't determine what the cause of death was.

Unfortunately, Roger, who was still living at home, also got sick. He began complaining of stomach cramps and nausea. Roger, too, died, and doctors performed an autopsy and discovered that his liver and kidneys had been completely destroyed.

The doctors, now suspicious of the cause of the deaths, sent samples from Roger's body to the Georgia State Crime Laboratory. The experts at the crime lab conducted dozens of tests and found that the samples contained high levels of arsenic. This evidence gave the authorities cause to dig up Rogers' brothers and son and test them.

Arrest and Mental Illness

Janie Lou Gibbs was arrested shortly after the autopsy on Roger's body was complete. At the time of her arrest in 1967 she was deemed not competent to stand trial. Instead, she was sent to a mental institution, where she stayed until 1974.

In 1974 Gibbs was deemed competent for trial, so she was charged with five counts of first-degree murder. She was tried, convicted, and sentenced to life imprisonment for her crimes in 1978.

Gibbs stayed in prison until April 1999, when she was found to be suffering from Parkinson's disease. Since prison authorities could no longer care for her, Gibbs was released into the custody of her brother and sent to a nursing home. She died in the nursing home in 2010. At the time of her death, Gibbs was considered clinically insane.

A Classic Black Widow

Janie Lou Gibbs was a classic black widow, who valued money more than her family. The motive for her killing sprees was simple; she wanted the insurance payments. Authorities estimated that Gibbs collected around $31,000 from the insurance company.

Prosecutors estimated that Gibbs tithed about 10% of the insurance money, or $3,100, to her church. Perhaps she thought that she could buy forgiveness for her crimes.

Gibbs was following in the footsteps of classic 19th century poisoners, such as the Black Widows of Liverpool. Like them, she derived her weapon of choice from a common household item. In Gibbs' case, it was rat poison, which was for sale at the local hardware store.

STACEY CASTOR: ANTIFREEZE POISONING MONSTER

Stacey Castor is one of most frightening and reprehensible female killers of all time. Not only did she poison two husbands, but when evidence mounted against her, Castor tried to murder and frame her own daughter.

The worst part of Stacey Castor's crimes was that she was able to get away with one murder and left free to commit another one. Worst of all, she was in a position to threaten the life of her daughter. It took years for authorities to uncover Stacey's crimes and put a stop to her.

The Black Widow from Upstate New York

Stacey Castor was a life resident of Clay, a small town in upstate New York. She met her first husband, Michael Wallace, when she was 17. The two married young, but their lives went nowhere; Michael made a poor living as a mechanic.

The two did have two daughters, Ashley and Bree, with whom Stacey apparently had a close relationship. The Wallaces lived quietly in their rural community until 1999. In that year Michael became very sick over the holiday season and died in early 2000.

Nobody could understand why a healthy and active man like Michael Wallace had become so sick. Relatives encouraged Wallace to get medical help but he refused. When Wallace died, his death was ruled a heart attack; he was only 38. Stacey was able to get away with it even though some people, including Wallace's sister, were getting suspicious of her.

Marrying and Killing Again

Stacey Wallace married a coworker named David Castor in 2003. Castor wasn't as lucky as Wallace had been; he would be dead in less than two years of the same cause: poisoning.

David Castor's death in 2005 was so unusual that it caused the police and the coroner to take a close look at Stacey. Incredibly, it was Stacy who called the local sheriff's department to her home because she couldn't open her husband's bedroom door. When the deputies arrived, they kicked in the door and found David Castor dead. Stacy at first claimed he had died of a heart attack then changed her story and claimed that Castor had committed suicide by drinking antifreeze.

The coroner went along with this story, which left Stacey free to bury Castor's body. In a bizarre twist, Castor was buried in a grave next to Michael Wallace. The death was so unusual that detectives suspected Stacey of murder.

Trying to Poison Her Own Daughter

Any thoughts that Stacey had of getting away with it were soon disproved. Detectives found evidence that David Castor was force-fed the antifreeze that killed him with a turkey baster. Police think Stacey filled the baster with the poison then stuffed it down his throat. They also exhumed Michael Wallace's body and had an autopsy conducted; tests showed that Wallace had died of antifreeze poisoning just like Castor had.

If that vicious murder wasn't enough, Stacey, now realizing that the law was closing in, devised an even more horrendous plan. The investigation dragged into September 2007; when the true extent of Stacey's evil was revealed, she made an attempt to kill her eldest daughter, Ashley. Castor hoped that she could plant enough evidence to frame Ashley then kill the girl to cover her tracks.

This time the poison was a mixture of alcohol and various drugs. Stacey tried to prove she was Ashley's friend by sitting down with her for a drink. The drink was booze laced with drugs. The drink knocked Ashley out, and Stacey left her on her bed to die, but the plan failed. Seventeen hours later, Ashley's sister Bree discovered the unconscious girl and called 911; paramedics arrived and saved her life. Castor gave the paramedics a suicide note that she had typed.

Arrest and Legal Maneuverings

Stacey Castor was arrested shortly after the attempt on Ashley's life. By then police had amassed a large amount of evidence and determined a motive for David's murder. They had discovered that David Castor was planning to change his will to keep Stacey and her daughters from inheriting his $300,000 estate.

Castor's arrest launched a series of legal battles that continue to this day. The prosecution won the opening round of the legal war in 2009 when Stacey Castor was convicted of second-degree murder and attempted second-degree murder. She was apparently never tried or convicted for Michael Wallace's death. Stacey was sentenced to 25 years to life in jail for killing David and another 25 years to life for attempting to kill Ashley.

Both Castor's attorneys and the prosecutors appealed the conviction. Those appeals are still being heard by courts in New York State. In a weird related move, David Castor's stepson David Castor Jr. and Castor's ex-wife Janice Poissant sued Stacey Castor, claiming she had stolen David's estate from them. The two also claimed that a couple named Lynn and Paul Pulaski had helped Stacey steal David's money.

In December 2011 Judge Anthony Paris ordered Stacey Castor and the Pulaskis to pay David Castor Jr. and his mother $277,118 in damages. It isn't clear if Stacey Castor can pay this amount. It's doubtful that she can make that kind of money at New York's Bedford Hills Correctional Facility for Women.

SUSAN SMITH: THE FAMILY DESTROYER WHO SHOCKED A NATION

Susan Smith made herself one of the most hated women in history by making a horrific crime more reprehensible. Not only did Smith kill her sons, an infant and a toddler, she also tried to stoke racial tensions by lying about it. Worst of all, her crimes were apparently motivated by selfishness and a complete indifference to human life and others.

The sheer callousness of Smith's crimes and the cold-blooded way in which she went about them are what shocked the nation. She put her small Southern hometown on the map and introduced the nation to a particularly loathsome new kind of monster, the woman who kills her own children. Worst of all, she did it simply because the children were in her way.

Lonely Little Girl from a Troubled Family

Susan Smith spent most of her life in the poor South Carolina mill town of Union. Smith grew up in a dysfunctional family with an alcoholic father who was constantly threatening to kill his wife and children. Some reports indicate that Smith's father, Harry Vaughn, was psychotic and obsessed with the idea that his wife was cheating on him.

The family was so troubled that Smith's half-brother, Michael Vaughn, tried to hang himself. Michael was eventually taken away by authorities and placed in a hospital. Harry Vaughn eventually committed suicide in 1978, shortly after his wife finally divorced him.

Harry Vaughn's death enabled Susan's mother, Linda, to climb the social ladder by marrying a local big wig named Beverly Russell. He was a successful businessman and an influential member of the Republican Party, which controlled the state and local governments. Yet all wasn't happy. Susan would claim that Beverly Russell had molested her and treated her with disdain.

Marriage and Suicide

Susan's troubles escalated in high school. She had an affair with an older married co-worker at the Winn-Dixie supermarket where she worked. Susan became pregnant, had an abortion, and tried to commit suicide with a drug overdose.

Shortly after graduating high school, Susan, now pregnant, married David Smith, a co-worker at Winn-Dixie. The marriage went badly because the young couple was poor and often in conflict with Susan's mother. They divorced in 1992 while Susan was pregnant with her second child, Alexander.

After Alexander's birth, Susan found a new job at the largest company in town, Conso Products, a textile mill. Susan worked as a bookkeeper and an assistant to the secretary of J. Carey Findlay, the company's CEO. Findlay had a rich and handsome son named Tom, who was single. Susan soon started sleeping with Tom Findlay and planning to marry him.

A Bizarre Life Leads to Murder

By 1994, Susan Smith was living a bizarre double life. She was a doting mother, yet she was reportedly having affairs with three men. She was having sex with her ex-husband David, Tom Findlay, and some rumors indicate her stepfather, Beverly Russell.

The strange double life came crashing down on Oct. 17, 1994, when Findlay sent her a sort of 'Dear John' letter breaking off their affair. In the letter, Findlay called Susan a good person, but said he wanted nothing more to do with her. It was this cold-blooded rejection that sent Susan Smith over the edge. In the letter, Tom admitted that he considered Susan beneath him because of her working class background. Findlay also mentioned the fact that he didn't want to marry a woman with children.

That night, after normal activities, such as a day of work and dinner with friends at a local restaurant, Susan Smith went home. She placed her sons in the car and took them for a drive. Susan drove to a boat ramp at nearby John D. Long Lake, then let the car run into the water with the boys strapped in their seats. The boys drowned and Susan wandered off.

Lies and a More Lies

Susan Smith's next actions were even more cold-blooded. She walked to a nearby home and told the residents that a black man had hijacked her car and kidnaped her sons. The residents called 911 and the sheriff's department was alerted. The local sheriff, Howard Wells, who oddly enough knew Susan and was reportedly a friend of her brother, Scotty Vaughn, took charge of the investigation.

Wells had his deputies search for the boys and Susan's car, a Mazda. He also asked the State of Law Enforcement (or SLED) for help. SLED sent a helicopter with sophisticated sensors to search John D. Long Lake and the nearby national forest. Divers began searching the lake, but found nothing.

By then, the media had learned of the case and reporters were streaming into Union to cover the story. Even though a media firestorm had erupted, investigators were getting suspicious of Susan – a description of the black man she gave police sounded cartoonish.

The Lies Come Home to Roost

By Oct. 27, 1994, Sheriff Wells was getting suspicious of Susan Smith and her story. He called in an expert, David Caldwell, the Director of SLED's Forensic Sciences Laboratory. Caldwell and FBI agents questioned Smith and gave her a lie detector test. When the results of the polygraph were positive, the investigators placed Susan under arrest.

The investigators did this because interviews showed that Susan's story was a lie. She claimed to have visited a Walmart parking lot with the children, but nobody remembered seeing them. Investigators had also learned about Susan's affair with Findlay.

By this time, the media, which had been portraying Smith as a victim, turned on her viciously. Reporters began pointing out the obvious inconsistencies in her story and digging up the sordid details of her personal life. Faced with the pressure from all sides, Smith collapsed and confessed to the crime. She told investigators where to find her boys.

Investigators went to the boat ramp at John D. Long Lake on Nov. 4, where they discovered the Mazda and the boys' bodies. The Mazda with Alexander and Michael still strapped in their seats was pulled from the water. Autopsies confirmed that the boys had been alive when they hit the water.

Still in Prison

Susan Smith was convicted of murder in 1995, but spared the death penalty; instead, she was sentenced to life in prison. The jury failed to believe her insanity defense. Smith is still in state prison in South Carolina and will remain there for years to come – she won't be eligible for parole until 2024.

Since she went to prison, Smith has attracted some notoriety. Media reports indicate that prison guards got in trouble for having sex with her behind bars. Outside the walls, Susan Smith remains a symbol of evil to a troubled nation.

RUTH ELLIS: THE LAST WOMAN HANGED IN ENGLAND

Being the last woman hanged in the United Kingdom wasn't Ruth Ellis's only claim to fame. The murderess and tabloid darling was one of the most colorful female murderers of all time. Her story was so dramatic and sensational that it inspired movies and changed British law and society.

Ellis's drama played out at a tumultuous time in British history when social mores were changing and the nation was adjusting to the fall of the Empire. Her story was at the center of the jaded and wild nightlife of 1950s London. Ellis operated in a shadowy world of nightclubs where gangsters and black marketers hobnobbed with celebrities, nobility, and politicians.

The debauchery and drunkenness in the colorful clubs contrasted dramatically with the dull existence of average Britons in the post-World War II era. Ellis's life and death made her as much a symbol of an era in British history as a celebrity murderer.

The Catholic Girl from Wales

Ironically enough, the future party girl who would be noted for her wild ways and good looks was born in a strict Catholic family in Wales. Her father, Arthur Hormby (or Arthur Neilson), was a musician who played in the bands on transatlantic ocean liners. Her mother was a Belgian immigrant.

The strict Catholic life didn't appeal to Ruth, who left school to work as a waitress when she was 14. The family moved to London in 1941, probably because World War II had ended transatlantic liner service and Arthur Neilson's job. The capitol was filled with Allied troops preparing for the invasion of Europe. Ruth became a V-Girl (a young lady who provided sexual favors to servicemen), and by the age of 17 she was pregnant by a Canadian soldier who disappeared into the fog of war.

Ruth Ellis ventured far from her Catholic roots in London - she became a nightclub hostess and worked as a nude model. This work brought her into contact with the underworld because the nightclubs were run by the gangsters who controlled the city's black market. By 1950, Ellis became a prostitute and had at least one illegal abortion.

London in the 1950s

Ruth Neilson became Ruth Ellis in 1950 when she married a dentist named George Ellis. He had been one of Ruth's customers when she was a prostitute. The dentist was an alcoholic who abused his wife and cheated on her.

Even though her marriage fell apart, Ruth succeeded in other fields. She had a small role in a British film called Lady Godiva Rides Again. She had a daughter named Georgina, but the birth ended her marriage. Ellis probably left her because he thought Georgina was fathered by somebody else.

By 1953 Ruth Ellis was managing a nightclub and attracting a lot of attention from glamorous men. Her suitors included the famous racecar driver Mike Hawthorn and his friend David Blakely. Ellis fell in love with the dashing upper class Blakely and even got pregnant by him, but aborted the baby when she realized he wouldn't give up his playboy ways for her.

Love Triangle and Murder

It was a love triangle that eventually led Ruth Ellis to murder. By 1955 Ellis was the mistress of Desmond Cussen, a wealthy businessman, but she was still involved with Blakely. Around this time Blakely asked Ruth to marry him, but then because abusive and punched Ruth in the chest when she was pregnant. This act caused Ruth to miscarry her baby.

On Easter Sunday 1955, Ruth Ellis decided to get her revenge on David Blakely. Ruth went looking for Blakely with a .38 caliber Smith & Wesson revolver. She found his car parked outside a pub called the Magdela in the London neighborhood of Hampstead and waited for him.

Around 9:30 p.m., Blakely and one of his mates came out of the pub. As the racer fumbled around his keys, Ruth opened fire. Her first shot missed, so she moved in for the kill and shot Blakely in the back at point-blank range. After Blakely fell she stood over him and kept pumping bullets into his body until the gun was empty.

The Case that Turned Britain Upside Down

An off-duty police constable who happened to be in the area walked up to Ellis and took the gun from her. He then placed the shooter under arrest and took her to the police station. After questioning, Ellis was booked for the crime and charged in magistrate's court.

Ruth Ellis's trial and execution were among the most famous and controversial in British history. Even though prosecutors had little trouble convincing a jury that Ellis was guilty and securing a death penalty against her, the decision was controversial. Many members of the public thought Ellis's actions were justified, but British law at the time had no exceptions for crimes of passion or killings committed in rage.

Many people, including the presiding judge, thought Ellis's death sentence was unreasonable. The case was even discussed in the cabinet, but the Home Secretary (the British cabinet minister with the power to grant pardons) refused to intervene.

The Hanging that Ended Britain's Death Penalty

Britain's celebrity hangman Albert Pierrepoint put the rope around Ruth's neck on July 13, 1955. Pierrepoint was already famous at the time for having hanged several other celebrity criminals, including Nazi war criminal Irma Grese, Acid Bath Murderer John George Haugh, and radio propagandist Lord Haw-Haw (a.k.a. William Joyce, the most notorious British traitor of World War II).

The hanging was unpopular and widely viewed as a miscarriage of justice. Around 50,000 people signed a petition to the Home Secretary asking for it to be stopped. The public clamor couldn't save Ruth Ellis, but led Her Majesty's Government to stop hanging in 1964 and end the death penalty as a punishment for murder in 1965. No other women were hanged in Britain after the outrage over Ruth's death.

Since her death Ruth Ellis's life has inspired movies, stage plays, and TV shows. There were unsuccessful efforts to get Ruth's conviction overturned and win her a pardon in the early 21st century. What good these efforts would have done for the woman fifty years after her death is unclear.

Ruth Ellis continued to inspire attention and hatred long after her death. In 1982, her son Andy (whom she had abandoned) destroyed Ruth's tombstone shortly before committing suicide. Ruth Ellis will keep attracting attention long after her hanging.

DELPHINE LALAURIE: THE MONSTER OF OLD NEW ORLEANS

No American city seems to have more legends or ghost stories than New Orleans. None of the stories of old New Orleans are more terrifying than those of a socialite named Delphine LaLaurie. If the legends are to be believed, Madam LaLaurie not only imprisoned and tortured her servants, she may have murdered two husbands.

LaLaurie's behavior was so brutal that it outraged the citizens of a city where slavery was considered an acceptable institution. Her actions laid bare the ugly atrocities that often went underneath the gentility and refinement of the old south.

Madam LaLaurie's wickedness became so infamous that her mansion at 1140 Royal Street is now regarded as a prominent New Orleans landmark and tourist attraction. Almost two centuries after Madam LaLaurie committed her crimes, people still come to visit her house and her story.

From Social Prominence to Infamy

Delphine LaLaurie was born in 1775 when New Orleans was still part of the Spanish Empire. Her parent's family, the Macartys, was a prominent one in the city's ruling classes. Delphine Macarty was prominent enough to marry important Spanish official Don Ramon Lopez y Angullo. On a trip to Spain in 1804, Delphine was even presented to that nation's Queen.

Don Ramon died in Havana and Delphine returned to New Orleans, which was now part of the United States because of the Louisiana Purchase. She married Jean Blanque, a banker, lawyer, and important local politician. Delphine had four children by Blanque, who died in 1816. After his death, Delphine married a much younger man, a doctor named Leonard Nicolas LaLaurie.

It was LaLaurie who helped Delphine build the mansion at 1140 Royal Street, which would later be revealed as a house of horrors. Delphine LaLaurie had become one of the city's most prominent socialites. The house she built was a three-story mansion, complete with slave quarters.

A Private House of Horrors

Details of exactly what was going on at 1140 Royal Street in the early 19th century are hard to find. What is known is that the brutalities inflicted on LaLaurie's slaves were so terrible that they inspired generations of ghost stories, pulp novels, and legends.

It is known that around 1832, a slave girl named Lia jumped from the mansion's roof to avoid punishment. The punishments being inflicted on the slaves were so brutal that Lia preferred suicide to her mistress's "care." Witnesses claimed that they saw Madame LaLaurie chasing Lia before her jump. Delphine apparently took after Lia because the girl had done a poor job of combing her mistress's hair.

The incident with Lia prompted authorities to investigate and eventually remove nine of LaLaurie's slaves from the home. The reason given for this action was the mistreatment the slaves were receiving. Stories began circulating that LaLaurie kept her cook chained to the stove (which must have been unbearable in the heat of New Orleans). Madame LaLaurie also reportedly beat her own daughters when the girls tried to feed the slaves.

The Fire and the Lynch Mob

The real exposure of the horrors came in 1834 when a slave, the cook who had been chained to the stove, set the LaLaurie mansion on fire. It isn't clear why the slave did this – she may have been trying to cover an escape attempt, get revenge, or commit suicide.

The fire caused a crowd of onlookers to enter the house to try and rescue the residents. The rescuers wondered why LaLaurie's slaves didn't flee the burning structure. They soon found their answer – all the slaves were chained up on upper floors of the building. Another slave told the police who came to investigate that LaLaurie often took slaves to a room from which they never returned.

In the room from which slaves never returned authorities found seven horribly mutilated African Americans. LaLaurie was deliberately chaining slaves up and torturing them. Some of the slaves said that they had been chained up for months. The slaves were taken to the city jail and put on display for everybody to see.

The slaves were so badly mauled that they inspired the formation of a lynch mob. A large mob gathered near LaLaurie's house and started talking about stringing her up – in other words, hanging her.

Escape and the Beginning of a Legend

The members of the mob never got to hang Madam LaLaurie. Having heard the lynch talk, she jumped into her carriage and drove to a waiting schooner as fast as she could. The schooner sailed away and the Madam was never seen again. Rumor had it that she fled to Mobile, Ala., and later to Paris, where she died at some unknown date. A grave with her name was discovered in a Paris cemetery in 1888.

Madam LaLaurie entered the world of folklore when writers learned of her story. They embellished the cruelty with claims that flesh had been sliced away, brains had been sucked out, and voodoo rites held in the house. Some writers have claimed that LaLaurie was really a vampire who was feeding on her slaves.

The real horror though was slavery itself. Madam LaLaurie's brutalities were typical of the tortures inflicted on slaves in the Old South. What made her atrocities different was that they occurred in the heart of a large city, rather than on an isolated plantation. Even though Madam LaLaurie was gone, the slaves of New Orleans would not see freedom until the Union forces occupied the city during the Civil War almost 30 years after Madam LaLaurie's house of horrors had exposed the truth about slavery for all to see.

DIANE DOWNS: THE MOTHER WHO SHOT HER OWN CHILDREN

The most frightening killers of all are those who seem to display two completely different personalities at different times. A prime example of this was Diane Downs, an Oregon mother who shot her own children, then tried to save the little ones by driving them to the emergency room.

Like Susan Smith, Diane Downs was outwardly a loving mother, but in reality, she was a completely selfish person who viewed her children as impediments to her social life. Downs was also mentally unhinged and separated from reality – she was obsessed with a married co-worker. Downs had the delusion that his man would leave his wife if her children were to disappear, so she made them disappear.

In another similarity with Susan Smith, Downs murdered her own children in cold blood and tried to blame the killing on an imaginary stranger. Downs was even more ruthless than Smith – she actually shot herself in an attempt to convince others that she had been attacked by somebody else.

Letter Carrier and Single Mom

Diane Downs was born and raised in Phoenix, Arizona; the only unusual thing about her childhood was claims that her father had molested her. Like many troubled young women, Downs tried to escape an unpleasant home life through marriage. In 1973, Downs married her high school sweetheart, Steven, just after he had left the Navy.

As often happens in such cases, young marital life deteriorated into a hell of hard work, low pay, and diminished expectations. The dream man Steve Downs turned out to be domineering and controlling. The couple worked at dead end jobs, including one building mobile homes. When the marriage didn't work out, Diane started having affairs with construction workers and any other man she ran into.

In 1979, Diane, who was still married to Steve, became pregnant with her third child, Danny, by a man other than her husband. Incredibly, Steve stuck with her and accepted Danny as his own. In

1981, Diane found a better job as a letter carrier for the U.S. Post Office in Chandler, Arizona. She also fell in love with a man named Lew Lewiston, but unlike Steve Downs, Lewiston had a sensible taste in women – he quickly walked out on Diane.

Move to Oregon and Murder

Like many troubled people, Diane Downs tried to escape her problems by moving to a completely different environment. During the early 1980s she packed up her children and moved to Central Oregon, where she worked at the Cottage Grove post office. Downs was still mentally unbalanced – she reportedly carried a .38 caliber handgun for protection on a mail route in small-town Oregon.

During this period Downs was trying to reconnect with another former lover, Robert Knickerbocker, who lived in Arizona. Like Lewiston, Knickerbocker sensibly ignored her overtures. It was probably Knickerbocker's rejections that drove her to kill her children.

The plan she conceived was both convoluted and cold-blooded: she would shoot her children and herself, and then try to blame the crime on a mysterious stranger.

Somebody Shot My Kids

Diane Downs put her horrendous plan into operation on May 19, 1983. On that day, she went to work, came home and picked up her kids, and went for a drive in the hills. Sometime during the drive, Diane stopped the car, got out her pistol, and shot all three of her children. The helpless kids were strapped into the seats of the car as she shot them.

Once that terrible drama had played out, Diane drove to a hospital in Springfield, Ore. At some point, she stopped the car and shot herself before continuing to the hospital. Once there, Diane started screaming that "somebody just shot my kids." Nurses ran out and found the three small children bleeding in the back seat.

Events then conspired to ruin Diane Downs's sick one-woman conspiracy. The first stroke of fate was a medical miracle – skilled surgeons and nurses managed to save the lives of the youngest child, Danny, and his oldest sister, Christie Ann. Their sister, Cheryl Lynn, wasn't so lucky – she was dead when Diane reached the hospital. The next event that trapped Diane Downs was some good old-fashioned police work.

Dick Tracy vs. Princess Die

Like Susan Smith, Diane Downs made up a story about a fictional carjacker. The difference was that Downs blamed a white man with long hair, while Smith blamed a black man. The problem for Diane was that detectives didn't believe her story for one minute.

The lead detective, who shared the name of Dick Tracy with the famed comic strip detective, was immediately suspicious. Tracy was particularly suspicious when he discovered that Downs's first call in the hospital was to Robert Knickerbocker. He was also bothered by her demeanor – she didn't seem to care what had happened to her children.

Tracy's suspicions were further heightened by forensic evidence that showed the children were shot at close range from inside the car. This contradicted Downs's claims that the longhaired stranger had fired in the car windows. They also learned that Downs owned a gun and found out about her affairs. Further evidence came from Arizona by detectives who uncovered evidence of Downs's love life. Police didn't yet have enough evidence to move against Downs, but they were worried enough to place guards on Christie and Danny's hospital rooms to protect them from their own mother.

The End of Princess Die

Diane Downs left the hospital and returned to work at the post office. Detectives were also at work, preparing a case for the grand jury. The evidence convinced the grand jury, and on Feb. 28, 1984, Downs was handcuffed and taken away outside the post office where she worked. A large crowd of reporters was already on scene to cover the arrest of Downs.

The press was calling Downs "Princess Die" because of her name and similarities to Diana, the Princess of Wales who was then very much in the news. Princess Die was put on trial in May 1984 in Eugene, Ore. Almost everybody in the small city turned out to watch the trial and gawk at the paparazzi who had come up from Los Angeles for the media circus.

The jury found Diane Downs guilty of one count of attempted murder, one count of assault, and one count of murder. She was sentenced to life imprisonment. The circus atmosphere of the trial increased when Downs gave birth to a baby girl during the trial. The father of the baby named Amy was unknown.

Today, Princess Die is imprisoned in the Valley Prison for Women in Chowchilla, Calif. She was moved out of Oregon when it was found that state's prisons couldn't hold her. In 1987, Downs made a successful escape attempt, but was soon recaptured and returned to prison. Downs will eligible for parole again in 2020.

Downs's three surviving children, Amy, Danny, and Christie, were adopted by loving families. They are all grown up and living normal lives without their mother.

CONSTANCE KENT: THE FIRST CELEBRITY MURDER

Constance Kent was one of the first celebrity murderers to attract a great deal of media attention. Her story was also one of the most unusual and sensational murder mysteries of all time. The reason her crime attracted so much interest is easy to see; Constance stabbed her three-year-old stepbrother so violently that she almost cut his head off.

The discovery of the body of Francis "Saville" Kent inspired a media frenzy and investigation that some believe inspired the creation of mystery stories. The worst part of the crime was that Constance Kent got away with it. She was able to murder her stepbrother and escape. It was only years later that she confessed of her own volition.

A Troubled Family

Constance Kent was born in 1844 to a very troubled family. Her mother was mentally ill and unable to care for her ten children. To make matters worse, Constance's father was in love with the children's governess, Mary Drew Pratt, and not his wife. The family had to move at least twice because of gossip.

When Constance's mother died in 1852, Samuel married Mary, with whom he had several more children. The family wasn't a happy one, and Constance may have resented her stepmother and stepsiblings.

Eventually the Kents settled in Rode, a small village in Wiltshire, England. The family wasn't popular in the neighborhood because Samuel Kent abused his servants.

The Mutilated Boy in the Outhouse

The Kents became one of the most famous families in England on June 30, 1860, when it was noticed that three-year-old Saville was missing from his bed. The family started searching the grounds of their country house and called in neighbors to help.

Eventually two of the neighbors found Saville's body inside an outhouse on the property. The boy lay in a pool of blood on the floor, and his throat had been slit. When one of them picked up the body, the boy's head almost fell. The murder horrified the region and soon made the London newspapers.

Nobody knew what to make of the killing, but the local police suspected a family servant named Elizabeth Gough. Another popular rumor in the area claimed that Samuel Kent had murdered his own son and dumped him in the outhouse. Like the JonBenet Ramsey case over 130 years later, the rumors increased media attention.

The Newspapers and a Celebrity Detective

As often happens in high profile murder cases, the press and not the police started directing the course of the investigation. Newspapers began attacking the Wiltshire police and demanding more competent investigation.

Over a month after the case, on July 14, 1860, local authorities appealed to Britain's highest law enforcement official, the Home Secretary, for help. The Home Secretary dispatched one of Scotland Yard's most experienced gumshoes, Detective Inspector Jack Whicher, to look into the matter. Whicher was one of the first detectives at Scotland Yard and something of a celebrity. Some of his cases had attracted the attention of Charles Dickens and other prominent authors.

Whicher made a conclusion that wasn't very pretty. After meeting the Kents and looking over the crime scene, he decided that Constance Kent, then sixteen, was the culprit. Unfortunately, there was no evidence linking Constance to the killing. All Whicher had to go on were his suspicions, which were not believed by the local judge or magistrate. In those days British police needed approval from a magistrate to make an arrest.

She Got Away with It

When he finished his investigation, Whicher admitted that the only way Constance Kent would ever get caught was if she confessed. Unfortunately, Whicher, unlike modern police, couldn't simply bring her in and break her down through questioning. Kent walked free and three years later moved out of the house.

Ironically enough, it was Constance Kent's strong Christian faith that proved her undoing. Kent moved to Brighton and lived in a religious establishment, a sort of nunnery, for a time. Eventually she confessed her crime to a priest named Arthur Wagner. Wagner was an Anglican (Church of England), but he followed the rules of the Roman Catholic Church.

Wagner couldn't go to the authorities without violating sacramental confession. Instead, he talked Kent into surrendering to the authorities. On April 25, 1865, Constance Kent and Arthur Wagner walked into the Bow Street Magistrate's Court in London and asked to see the magistrate.

Once they were alone with the magistrate Constance confessed to the crime. She told the magistrate that she had murdered her stepbrother out of hatred for her stepmother. Based on her confession, Constance Kent was convicted of murder and sentenced to death.

The World's Oldest Ex-Murderer

Constance Kent's confession was too late to save the career of Jack Whicher; he had been forced to retire in 1864 largely because of his failure in the Kent case. Constance Kent was saved from the hangman by Queen Victoria, who commuted her sentence to life in prison.

Constance was released from prison in 1885 and seemed to disappear. In reality, she immigrated to Australia in 1886. Constance Kent lived in Australia under the name Emily Kaye for nearly sixty years. She died in that country in 1944, when she was over 100 years old. Interestingly enough, nobody realized that Constance Kent had moved to Australia and died there until many years her death.

www.ingramcontent.com/pod-product-compliance
Lightning Source LLC
Chambersburg PA
CBHW020250030426
42336CB00010B/707